THE COMPLETE GREEK TRAGEDIES

Edited by David Grene and Richmond Lattimore

SOPHOCLES · I

OEDIPUS THE KING
Translated by David Grene

OEDIPUS AT COLONUS
Translated by Robert Fitzgerald

ANTIGONE
Translated by Elizabeth Wyckoff

With an Introduction by
DAVID GRENE

THE UNIVERSITY OF CHICAGO PRESS

CHICAGO & LONDON

International Standard Book Number: 0–226–30785–9

Library of Congress Catalog Card Number: 54–10731

THE UNIVERSITY OF CHICAGO PRESS, CHICAGO 60637
The University of Chicago Press, Ltd., London

TABLE OF CONTENTS

INTRODUCTION

"The Theban Plays" by Sophocles

THIS series of plays, *Oedipus the King, Oedipus at Colonus,* and *Antigone,* was written over a wide interval of years. The dating is only approximate, for reliable evidence is lacking; but the *Antigone* was produced in 441 B.C. when Sophocles was probably fifty-four, and *Oedipus the King* some fourteen or fifteen years later. *Oedipus at Colonus* was apparently produced the year after its author's death at the age of ninety in 405 B.C. Thus, although the three plays are concerned with the same legend, they were not conceived and executed at the same time and with a single purpose, as is the case with Aeschylus' *Oresteia.* We can here see how a story teased the imagination of Sophocles until it found its final expression. We can see the degrees of variation in treatment he gave the myth each time he handled it. And perhaps we can come to some notion of what the myths meant to Sophocles as raw material for the theater.

The internal dramatic dates of the three plays do not agree with the order of their composition. As far as the legend is concerned, the story runs in sequence: *Oedipus the King, Oedipus at Colonus, Antigone.* But Sophocles wrote them in the order: *Antigone, Oedipus the King, Oedipus at Colonus.* In view of this and the long interval between the composition of the individual plays, we would expect some inconsistencies between the three versions. And there are fairly serious inconsistencies—in facts, for instance. At the conclusion of *Oedipus the King,* Creon is in undisputed authority after the removal of Oedipus. Though he appeals to him to look after his daughters, Oedipus refrains from asking Creon to do anything for his sons, who, he says, will be all right on their own (*OK* 1460). It is Creon who will succeed Oedipus in Thebes, and there is no question of any legitimate claim of Oedipus' descendants (*OK* 1418). But in *Antig-one,* Creon tells the chorus that he has favorably observed their loyalty first to Oedipus and then to his sons, and so has hope of their devotion to himself. In *Oedipus at Colonus*—the last of the three plays he wrote—Sophocles makes one of his very few clumsy efforts to patch the discrepancies together. In *Oedipus at Colonus* (ll. 367 ff.), Ismene says that *at first* the two sons were willing to leave the throne to Creon in view of their fatal family heritage, but after a while they decided to take over the monarchy and the quarrel was only between themselves as to who should succeed. At this point Creon has vanished out of the picture altogether! Again, the responsibility for the decision to expel Oedipus from Thebes and keep him out rests, in *Oedipus the King,* entirely with Creon, who announces that he will consult Apollo in the matter. In *Oedipus at Colonus* his sons' guilt in condemning their father to exile is one of the bitterest counts in Oedipus' indictment of them (*OC* 1360 ff.). These are important differences. We do not know anything really certain about the manner of publication of the plays after their production. We know even less about Sophocles' treatment of his own scripts. Maybe he simply did not bother to keep them after he saw them as far as the stage, though that seems unlikely. Or it is possible and likelier that Sophocles, as he wrote the last play in extreme old age and in what seems to be the characteristic self-absorption of the last years of his life, cared little about whether *Oedipus at Colonus* exactly tallied, in its presentation, with the stories he had written thirty-seven and twenty-two years earlier.

Let us for the moment disregard the details of the story and concentrate on what would seem to be the central theme of the first two plays in order of composition. And here we find something very curious. Most critics have felt the significance of the *Antigone* to lie in the opposition of Creon and Antigone and all that this opposition represents. It is thus a play about something quite different from *Oedipus the King.* And yet what a remarkable similarity there is in the dilemma of Creon in *Antigone* and Oedipus himself in the first Oedipus play. In both of them a king has taken a decision which is disobeyed or questioned by his subjects. In both, the ruler misconstrues the role of the rebel and his own as a sovereign. In both, he has a crucial encounter with the priest Teiresias, who warns him that the forces of religion are against him. In both, he charges that the priest has been suborned. There the resemblance ends; for, after abusing the old prophet, Creon is overcome with fear of his authority and, too late, tries to undo his mistake. In *Oedipus the King* the king defies all assaults upon his decision until the deadly self-knowledge which starts to work in him has accomplished its course and he is convicted out of his own mouth.

Usually, as we know, the *Antigone* is interpreted entirely as the conflict between Creon and Antigone. It has often been regarded as the classical statement of the struggle between the law of the individual conscience and the central power of the state. Unquestionably, these issues are inherent in the play. Unquestionably, even, Sophocles would understand the modern way of seeing his play, for the issue of the opposition of the individual and the state was sufficiently present to his mind to make this significant for him. But can the parallelism between the position of Oedipus in the one play and Creon in the other be quite irrelevant to the interpretation of the two? And is it not very striking that such a large share of the *Antigone* should be devoted to the conclusion of the conflict, as far as Creon is concerned, and to the destruction of his human happiness?

What I would suggest is this: that Sophocles had at the time of writing the first play (in 442 B.C.) a theme in mind which centered in the Theban trilogy. One might express it by saying that it is the story of a ruler who makes a mistaken decision, though in good faith, and who then finds himself opposed in a fashion which he misunderstands and which induces him to persist in his mistake. This story is later on going to be that of a man who breaks divine law without realizing that he is doing so, and whose destruction is then brought about by the voice of the divine law in society. Between the *Antigone* and *Oedipus the King,* the theme has developed further, for in the latter play Sophocles is showing how the ruler who breaks the divine law may, for all he can see and understand, be entirely innocent, but nonetheless his guilt is an objective fact. In the third play, *Oedipus at Colonus,* this issue reaches its final statement. The old Oedipus is admittedly a kind of monster. Wherever he comes, people shrink from him. Yet his guilt carries with it some sort of innocence on which God will set his seal. For the old man is both cursed and blessed. The god gives him an extraordinary end, and the last place of his mortal habitation is blessed forever.

What this interpretation would mean, if correct, is that Sophocles started to write about the Theban legend, the story of Oedipus and his children, without having fully understood what he wanted to say about it. He may have been, and probably was, drawn, unknown to himself, to the dramatization of this particular legend because in it lay the material of the greatest theme of his later artistic life. But first he tried his hand at it in the opposition of Creon and Antigone. However, even while he did this, the character of Creon and his role in the play were shaping what was to be the decisive turn in the story he was going to write—the Oedipus saga.

Thus there is a certain elasticity in the entire treatment of myth. The author will accent a certain character at one time to suit a play and change the accent to suit another. Or he may even discover the same theme in a different myth. This is suggested by a short comparison of the *Philoctetes* and *Oedipus at Colonus,* both written in the last few years of Sophocles' life. The figure of Philoctetes, though occurring in a totally different legend from Oedipus, is a twin child with Oedipus in Sophocles' dramatic imagination. In both these plays, the *Philoctetes* and *Oedipus at Colonus,* the hero is a man whose value is inextricably coupled with his offensive quality. Philoctetes is the archer whose bow will overcome Troy. He is also the creature whose stinking infested wound moves everyone to disgust who has to do with him. Oedipus is accursed in the sight of all men; he had committed the two crimes, parricide and incest, which rendered him an outcast in any human society. But he is also the one to whom, at his end, God will give the marks of his favor, and the place where he is last seen on earth will be lucky and blessed. This combination of the evil and the good is too marked, in these two plays, to be accidental. It is surely the idea which inspired the old Sophocles for his two last plays. There is, however, an important further development of the theme in the *Oedipus at Colonus.* For there in Oedipus' mind the rational innocence—the fact that he had committed the offenses unknowingly—is, for him at least, important in God's final justification of him. Sophocles is declaring that the sin of Oedipus is real; that the consequences in the form of the loneliness, neglect, and suffering of the years of wandering are inevitable; but that the will and the consciousness are also some measure of man's sin—and when the sinner sinned necessarily and unwittingly, his suffering can be compensation enough for his guilt. He may at the end be blessed and a blessing. This is not the same doctrine as that of Aeschylus, when he asserts that through suffering comes wisdom. Nor is it the Christian doctrine of a man purified by suffering as by fire. Oedipus in his contact with Creon, in his interview with Polyneices shows himself as bitter, sudden in anger, and implacable as ever. He is indeed a monstrous old man. But at the last, he is, in a measure, *vindicated*. Yet in *Philoctetes* the theme of the union of the offensive and the beneficial, which in *Oedipus at Colonus* becomes the curse and the blessing, is seen without the addition of conscious innocence and unconscious guilt. Can we say that Sophocles finally felt that the consciousness of innocence in Oedipus is the balancing factor in the story? That in this sense *Oedipus at Colonus* is the further step beyond *Philoctetes* in the clarification of the dramatic subject which occupied the very old author? Or that the consciousness of innocence when linked with objective guilt is only the human shield against the cruelty of the irrational—that Oedipus is meaningful in his combination of guilt and innocence as a manifestation of God and of destiny and that his explanation of his conscious innocence is only the poor human inadequate explanation? Everyone will answer this according to his own choice. But, clearly, the theme of Philoctetes and the theme of the old Oedipus are connected.

If an analysis such as this has importance, it is to show the relation of Sophocles to the raw material of his plays—the myth. It is to show the maturing of a theme in Sophocles' mind and his successive treatments of it in the same and different legends. In the Oedipus story it is a certain fundamental situation which becomes significant for Sophocles, and the characters are altered to suit the story. Creon in the first, Oedipus in the second, are examples of the same sort of dilemma, even though the dilemma of Creon in the *Antigone* is incidental to the main emphasis of the play, which is on Antigone. But the dilemma was to be much more fruitful for Sophocles as a writer and thinker than the plain issue between Antigone and Creon. The dilemma resolves itself in the last play at the end of Sophocles' life into the dramatic statement of a principle, of the union of the blessed and the cursed, of the just and the unjust, and sometimes (not always) of the consciously innocent and the unconsciously guilty. The fact that Sophocles could in two successive treatments of the play fifteen years apart switch the parts of Creon and Oedipus indicates that neither the moral color of the characters nor even their identity was absolutely fixed in his mind. The same conclusion is borne out by the great similarity between the *Philoctetes* and the *Oedipus at Colonus*. Sophocles in his last days was incessantly thinking of the man who is blessed and cursed. For the theater he became once the lame castaway Philoctetes, who yet, in virtue of his archery, is to be the conqueror of Troy; in the next play he is Oedipus, who sinned against the order of human society but is still to be the blessing of Athens and the patron saint of Colonus. It is the theme and not the man that matters. Consequently, it is the kernel of the legend, as he saw it for the moment, that is sacred for Sophocles, not the identification of all the characters in a certain relation to one another. True, he has treated the Oedipus story three times in his life, which means that the Oedipus story had a certain fascination for him—that somehow hidden in it he knew there was what he wanted to say. But he did not have to think of the whole story and the interdependence of its characters when he made his changes each time. One stage of the theme borne by the hero is given to a character in a totally different myth. The sequence is Creon, Oedipus, Philoctetes, Oedipus. It may seem absurd to link Creon, the obvious form of tyrant (as conceived by the Athenians), and Philoctetes. But it is the progression we should notice. The tyrant who with true and good intentions orders what is wrong, morally and religiously, is crudely represented in Creon; he is much more subtly represented in Oedipus himself in the next play. But the similarity of the situation and the nature of the opposition to him proves how generically the character is conceived. You can switch the labels, and Creon becomes Oedipus. But if the character is generic, the situation is deepening. We are beginning to understand *why* a certain sort of tyrant may be a tyrant and in a shadowy way how conscious and unconscious guilt are related. In the *Philoctetes* and *Oedipus at Colonus* the situation is being seen in its last stages. We are no longer concerned with how Philoctetes came to sin or how Oedipus is the author of his own ruin. But only how does it feel to be an object both of disgust and of fear to your fellows, while you yourself are simultaneously aware of the injustice of your treatment and at last, in *Oedipus at Colonus,* of the objective proofs of God's favor.

For Sophocles the myth was the treatment of the generic aspect of human dilemmas. What he made of the myth in his plays was neither history nor the kind of dramatic creation represented by *Hamlet* or *Macbeth*. Not history, for in no sense is the uniqueness of the event or the uniqueness of the character important; not drama in the Shakespearean sense, because Sophocles' figures do not have, as Shakespeare's do, the timeless and complete reality in themselves. Behind the figure of Oedipus or Creon stands the tyrant of the legend; and behind the tyrant of the legend, the meaning of all despotic authority. Behind the old Oedipus is the beggar and wanderer of the legend, and behind him the mysterious human combination of opposites—opposites in meaning and in fact. And so the character may fluctuate or the names may vary. It is the theme, the generic side of tragedy, which is important; it is there that the emphasis of the play rests.

DAVID GRENE

UNIVERSITY OF CHICAGO

OEDIPUS THE KING

Translated by David Grene

CHARACTERS

Oedipus, King of Thebes

Jocasta, His Wife

Creon, His Brother-in-Law

Teiresias, an Old Blind Prophet

A Priest

First Messenger

Second Messenger

A Herdsman

A Chorus of Old Men of Thebes

OEDIPUS THE KING

SCENE: *In front of the palace of Oedipus at Thebes. To the right of the stage near the altar stands the Priest with a crowd of children. Oedipus emerges from the central door.*

Oedipus

Children, young sons and daughters of old Cadmus,
why do you sit here with your suppliant crowns?
The town is heavy with a mingled burden
of sounds and smells, of groans and hymns and incense;   5
I did not think it fit that I should hear
of this from messengers but came myself,—
I Oedipus whom all men call the Great.

                        (*He turns to the Priest.*)

You're old and they are young; come, speak for them.
What do you fear or want, that you sit here   10
suppliant? Indeed I'm willing to give all
that you may need; I would be very hard
should I not pity suppliants like these.

Priest

O ruler of my country, Oedipus,
you see our company around the altar;   15
you see our ages; some of us, like these,
who cannot yet fly far, and some of us
heavy with age; these children are the chosen
among the young, and I the priest of Zeus.
Within the market place sit others crowned   20
with suppliant garlands, at the double shrine
of Pallas and the temple where Ismenus
gives oracles by fire. King, you yourself
have seen our city reeling like a wreck
already; it can scarcely lift its prow
out of the depths, out of the bloody surf.

A blight is on the fruitful plants of the earth, 25
A blight is on the cattle in the fields,
a blight is on our women that no children
are born to them; a God that carries fire,
a deadly pestilence, is on our town,
strikes us and spares not, and the house of Cadmus
is emptied of its people while black Death
grows rich in groaning and in lamentation. 30
We have not come as suppliants to this altar
because we thought of you as of a God,
but rather judging you the first of men
in all the chances of this life and when
we mortals have to do with more than man.
You came and by your coming saved our city, 35
freed us from tribute which we paid of old
to the Sphinx, cruel singer. This you did
in virtue of no knowledge we could give you,
in virtue of no teaching; it was God
that aided you, men say, and you are held
with God's assistance to have saved our lives.
Now Oedipus, Greatest in all men's eyes, 40
here falling at your feet we all entreat you,
find us some strength for rescue.
Perhaps you'll hear a wise word from some God,
perhaps you will learn something from a man
(for I have seen that for the skilled of practice
the outcome of their counsels live the most). 45
Noblest of men, go, and raise up our city,
go,—and give heed. For now this land of ours
calls you its savior since you saved it once.
So, let us never speak about your reign
as of a time when first our feet were set
secure on high, but later fell to ruin. 50
Raise up our city, save it and raise it up.
Once you have brought us luck with happy omen;
be no less now in fortune.

If you will rule this land, as now you rule it,
better to rule it full of men than empty. 55
For neither tower nor ship is anything
when empty, and none live in it together.

Oedipus

I pity you, children. You have come full of longing,
but I have known the story before you told it
only too well. I know you are all sick,
yet there is not one of you, sick though you are, 60
that is as sick as I myself.
Your several sorrows each have single scope
and touch but one of you. My spirit groans
for city and myself and you at once.
You have not roused me like a man from sleep; 65
know that I have given many tears to this,
gone many ways wandering in thought,
but as I thought I found only one remedy
and that I took. I sent Menoeceus' son
Creon, Jocasta's brother, to Apollo, 70
to his Pythian temple,
that he might learn there by what act or word
I could save this city. As I count the days,
it vexes me what ails him; he is gone
far longer than he needed for the journey. 75
But when he comes, then, may I prove a villain,
if I shall not do all the God commands.

Priest

Thanks for your gracious words. Your servants here
signal that Creon is this moment coming.

Oedipus

His face is bright. O holy Lord Apollo, 80
grant that his news too may be bright for us
and bring us safety.

Priest

    It is happy news,
    I think, for else his head would not be crowned
    with sprigs of fruitful laurel.

Oedipus

                We will know soon,
    he's within hail. Lord Creon, my good brother,   85
    what is the word you bring us from the God?

                            (Creon enters.)

Creon

    A good word,—for things hard to bear themselves
    if in the final issue all is well
    I count complete good fortune.

Oedipus

                What do you mean?
    What you have said so far
    leaves me uncertain whether to trust or fear.   90

Creon

    If you will hear my news before these others
    I am ready to speak, or else to go within.

Oedipus

    Speak it to all;
    the grief I bear, I bear it more for these
    than for my own heart.

Creon

                I will tell you, then,   95
    what I heard from the God.
    King Phoebus in plain words commanded us
    to drive out a pollution from our land,
    pollution grown ingrained within the land;
    drive it out, said the God, not cherish it,
    till it's past cure.

Oedipus

                What is the rite
    of purification? How shall it be done?

Creon

    By banishing a man, or expiation   100
    of blood by blood, since it is murder guilt
    which holds our city in this destroying storm.

Oedipus

    Who is this man whose fate the God pronounces?

Creon

    My Lord, before you piloted the state
    we had a king called Laius.

Oedipus

    I know of him by hearsay. I have not seen him.   105

Creon

    The God commanded clearly: let some one
    punish with force this dead man's murderers.

Oedipus

    Where are they in the world? Where would a trace
    of this old crime be found? It would be hard
    to guess where.

Creon

                  The clue is in this land;   110
    that which is sought is found;
    the unheeded thing escapes:
    so said the God.

Oedipus

                Was it at home,
    or in the country that death came upon him,
    or in another country travelling?

Creon

    He went, he said himself, upon an embassy,
    but never returned when he set out from home.   115

Oedipus

    Was there no messenger, no fellow traveller
    who knew what happened? Such a one might tell
    something of use.

Creon

> They were all killed save one. He fled in terror
> and he could tell us nothing in clear terms
> of what he knew, nothing, but one thing only.

Oedipus

> What was it?   120
> If we could even find a slim beginning
> in which to hope, we might discover much.

Creon

> This man said that the robbers they encountered
> were many and the hands that did the murder
> were many; it was no man's single power.

Oedipus

> How could a robber dare a deed like this
> were he not helped with money from the city,
> money and treachery?   125

Creon

>   That indeed was thought.
> But Laius was dead and in our trouble
> there was none to help.

Oedipus

> What trouble was so great to hinder you
> inquiring out the murder of your king?

Creon

> The riddling Sphinx induced us to neglect   130
> mysterious crimes and rather seek solution
> of troubles at our feet.

Oedipus

> I will bring this to light again. King Phoebus
> fittingly took this care about the dead,
> and you too fittingly.
> And justly you will see in me an ally,   135
> a champion of my country and the God.
> For when I drive pollution from the land

I will not serve a distant friend's advantage,
but act in my own interest. Whoever
he was that killed the king may readily
wish to dispatch me with his murderous hand;   140
so helping the dead king I help myself.

Come, children, take your suppliant boughs and go;
up from the altars now. Call the assembly
and let it meet upon the understanding
that I'll do everything. God will decide   145
whether we prosper or remain in sorrow.

Priest
     Rise, children—it was this we came to seek,
     which of himself the king now offers us.
     May Phoebus who gave us the oracle
     come to our rescue and stay the plague.   150

                         (*Exeunt all but the Chorus.*)

Chorus
     Strophe
     What is the sweet spoken word of God from the shrine of Pytho
          rich in gold
     that has come to glorious Thebes?
     I am stretched on the rack of doubt, and terror and trembling
          hold
     my heart, O Delian Healer, and I worship full of fears
     for what doom you will bring to pass, new or renewed in the 155
          revolving years.
     Speak to me, immortal voice,
     child of golden Hope.

     Antistrophe
     First I call on you, Athene, deathless daughter of Zeus,
     and Artemis, Earth Upholder,   160
     who sits in the midst of the market place in the throne which
          men call Fame,
     and Phoebus, the Far Shooter, three averters of Fate,

come to us now, if ever before, when ruin rushed upon the state,   165
you drove destruction's flame away
out of our land.

Strophe

Our sorrows defy number;
all the ship's timbers are rotten;
taking of thought is no spear for the driving away of the plague.   170
There are no growing children in this famous land;
there are no women bearing the pangs of childbirth.
You may see them one with another, like birds swift on the
   wing,   175
quicker than fire unmastered,
speeding away to the coast of the Western God.

Antistrophe

In the unnumbered deaths
of its people the city dies;
those children that are born lie dead on the naked earth
unpitied, spreading contagion of death; and grey haired mothers
   and wives
everywhere stand at the altar's edge, suppliant, moaning;   182–85
the hymn to the healing God rings out but with it the wailing
   voices are blended.
From these our sufferings grant us, O golden Daughter of Zeus,
glad-faced deliverance.

Strophe

There is no clash of brazen shields but our fight is with the War
   God,
a War God ringed with the cries of men, a savage God who burns   191
   us;
grant that he turn in racing course backwards out of our country's bounds
to the great palace of Amphitrite or where the waves of the   195
   Thracian sea
deny the stranger safe anchorage.
Whatsoever escapes the night

at last the light of day revisits;
so smite the War God, Father Zeus,
beneath your thunderbolt,
for you are the Lord of the lightning, the lightning that
    carries fire.   200

Antistrophe
And your unconquered arrow shafts, winged by the golden
    corded bow,
Lycean King, I beg to be at our side for help;   205
and the gleaming torches of Artemis with which she scours the
    Lycean hills,
and I call on the God with the turban of gold, who gave his name
    to this country of ours,   210
the Bacchic God with the wind flushed face,
Evian One, who travel
with the Maenad company,
combat the God that burns us
with your torch of pine;
for the God that is our enemy is a God unhonoured among the   215
    Gods.

                                (Oedipus returns.)

Oedipus
For what you ask me—if you will hear my words,
and hearing welcome them and fight the plague,
you will find strength and lightening of your load.

Hark to me; what I say to you, I say
as one that is a stranger to the story
as stranger to the deed. For I would not   220
be far upon the track if I alone
were tracing it without a clue. But now,
since after all was finished, I became
a citizen among you, citizens—
now I proclaim to all the men of Thebes:
who so among you knows the murderer   225
by whose hand Laius, son of Labdacus,

died—I command him to tell everything
to me,—yes, though he fears himself to take the blame
on his own head; for bitter punishment
he shall have none, but leave this land unharmed.
Or if he knows the murderer, another,   230
a foreigner, still let him speak the truth.
For I will pay him and be grateful, too.
But if you shall keep silence, if perhaps
some one of you, to shield a guilty friend,
or for his own sake shall reject my words—
hear what I shall do then: 235
I forbid that man, whoever he be, my land,
my land where I hold sovereignty and throne;
and I forbid any to welcome him
or cry him greeting or make him a sharer   240
in sacrifice or offering to the Gods,
or give him water for his hands to wash.
I command all to drive him from their homes,
since he is our pollution, as the oracle
of Pytho's God proclaimed him now to me.
So I stand forth a champion of the God
and of the man who died.   245
Upon the murderer I invoke this curse—
whether he is one man and all unknown,
or one of many—may he wear out his life
in misery to miserable doom!
If with my knowledge he lives at my hearth   250
I pray that I myself may feel my curse.
On you I lay my charge to fulfill all this
for me, for the God, and for this land of ours
destroyed and blighted, by the God forsaken.

Even were this no matter of God's ordinance   255
it would not fit you so to leave it lie,
unpurified, since a good man is dead
and one that was a king. Search it out.

Since I am now the holder of his office,
and have his bed and wife that once was his,   260
and had his line not been unfortunate
we would have common children—(fortune leaped
upon his head)—because of all these things,
I fight in his defence as for my father,
and I shall try all means to take the murderer   265
of Laius the son of Labdacus
the son of Polydorus and before him
of Cadmus and before him of Agenor.
Those who do not obey me, may the Gods
grant no crops springing from the ground they plough   270
nor children to their women! May a fate
like this, or one still worse than this consume them!
For you whom these words please, the other Thebans,
may Justice as your ally and all the Gods
live with you, blessing you now and for ever!   275

Chorus
    As you have held me to my oath, I speak:
    I neither killed the king nor can declare
    the killer; but since Phoebus set the quest
    it is his part to tell who the man is.

Oedipus
    Right; but to put compulsion on the Gods   280
    against their will—no man can do that.

Chorus
    May I then say what I think second best?

Oedipus
    If there's a third best, too, spare not to tell it.

Chorus
    I know that what the Lord Teiresias
    sees, is most often what the Lord Apollo   285
    sees. If you should inquire of this from him
    you might find out most clearly.

Oedipus
    Even in this my actions have not been sluggard.
    On Creon's word I have sent two messengers
    and why the prophet is not here already
    I have been wondering.

Chorus
                            His skill apart   290
    there is besides only an old faint story.

Oedipus
    What is it?
    I look at every story.

Chorus
                        It was said
    that he was killed by certain wayfarers.

Oedipus
    I heard that, too, but no one saw the killer.

Chorus
    Yet if he has a share of fear at all,
    his courage will not stand firm, hearing your curse.   295

Oedipus
    The man who in the doing did not shrink
    will fear no word.

Chorus
                        Here comes his prosecutor:
    led by your men the godly prophet comes
    in whom alone of mankind truth is native.

                        (*Enter Teiresias, led by a little boy.*)

Oedipus
    Teiresias, you are versed in everything,   300
    things teachable and things not to be spoken,
    things of the heaven and earth-creeping things.
    You have no eyes but in your mind you know
    with what a plague our city is afflicted.
    My lord, in you alone we find a champion,

in you alone one that can rescue us.
Perhaps you have not heard the messengers,   305
but Phoebus sent in answer to our sending
an oracle declaring that our freedom
from this disease would only come when we
should learn the names of those who killed King Laius,
and kill them or expel from our country.
Do not begrudge us oracles from birds,   310
or any other way of prophecy
within your skill; save yourself and the city,
save me; redeem the debt of our pollution
that lies on us because of this dead man.
We are in your hands; pains are most nobly taken
to help another when you have means and power.   315

Teiresias

Alas, how terrible is wisdom when
it brings no profit to the man that's wise!
This I knew well, but had forgotten it,
else I would not have come here.

Oedipus

What is this?
How sad you are now you have come!

Teiresias

Let me
go home. It will be easiest for us both   320
to bear our several destinies to the end
if you will follow my advice.

Oedipus

You'd rob us
of this your gift of prophecy? You talk
as one who had no care for law nor love
for Thebes who reared you.

Teiresias

Yes, but I see that even your own words
miss the mark; therefore I must fear for mine.   325

Oedipus

    For God's sake if you know of anything,
    do not turn from us; all of us kneel to you,
    all of us here, your suppliants.

Teiresias

    All of you here know nothing. I will not
    bring to the light of day my troubles, mine—
    rather than call them yours.

Oedipus

                  What do you mean?
    You know of something but refuse to speak.
    Would you betray us and destroy the city?   330

Teiresias

    I will not bring this pain upon us both,
    neither on you nor on myself. Why is it
    you question me and waste your labour? I
    will tell you nothing.

Oedipus

    You would provoke a stone! Tell us, you villain,   335
    tell us, and do not stand there quietly
    unmoved and balking at the issue.

Teiresias

    You blame my temper but you do not see
    your own that lives within you; it is me
    you chide.

Oedipus

    Who would not feel his temper rise
    at words like these with which you shame our city?   340

Teiresias

    Of themselves things will come, although I hide them
    and breathe no word of them.

Oedipus

                Since they will come
    tell them to me.

Teiresias
                    I will say nothing further.
Against this answer let your temper rage
as wildly as you will.

Oedipus
                    Indeed I am   345
so angry I shall not hold back a jot
of what I think. For I would have you know
I think you were complotter of the deed
and doer of the deed save in so far
as for the actual killing. Had you had eyes
I would have said alone you murdered him.

Teiresias
Yes? Then I warn you faithfully to keep   350
the letter of your proclamation and
from this day forth to speak no word of greeting
to these nor me; you are the land's pollution.

Oedipus
How shamelessly you started up this taunt!
How do you think you will escape?   355

Teiresias
                    I have.
I have escaped; the truth is what I cherish
and that's my strength.

Oedipus
                    And who has taught you truth?
Not your profession surely!

Teiresias
                    You have taught me,
for you have made me speak against my will.

Oedipus
Speak what? Tell me again that I may learn it better.

Teiresias
Did you not understand before or would you
provoke me into speaking?   360

Oedipus
> I did not grasp it,
not so to call it known. Say it again.

Teiresias
> I say you are the murderer of the king
whose murderer you seek.

Oedipus
> Not twice you shall
say calumnies like this and stay unpunished.

Teiresias
> Shall I say more to tempt your anger more?

Oedipus
> As much as you desire; it will be said   365
in vain.

Teiresias
> I say that with those you love best
you live in foulest shame unconsciously
and do not see where you are in calamity.

Oedipus
> Do you imagine you can always talk
like this, and live to laugh at it hereafter?

Teiresias
> Yes, if the truth has anything of strength.

Oedipus
> It has, but not for you; it has no strength   370
for you because you are blind in mind and ears
as well as in your eyes.

Teiresias
> You are a poor wretch
to taunt me with the very insults which
every one soon will heap upon yourself.

Oedipus
> Your life is one long night so that you cannot
hurt me or any other who sees the light.   375

Teiresias
> It is not fate that I should be your ruin,
> Apollo is enough; it is his care
> to work this out.

Oedipus
>   Was this your own design
> or Creon's?

Teiresias
>   Creon is no hurt to you,
> but you are to yourself.

Oedipus
> Wealth, sovereignty and skill outmatching skill   380
> for the contrivance of an envied life!
> Great store of jealousy fill your treasury chests,
> if my friend Creon, friend from the first and loyal,   385
> thus secretly attacks me, secretly
> desires to drive me out and secretly
> suborns this juggling, trick devising quack,
> this wily beggar who has only eyes
> for his own gains, but blindness in his skill.
> For, tell me, where have you seen clear, Teiresias,   390
> with your prophetic eyes? When the dark singer,
> the sphinx, was in your country, did you speak
> word of deliverance to its citizens?
> And yet the riddle's answer was not the province
> of a chance comer. It was a prophet's task
> and plainly you had no such gift of prophecy   395
> from birds nor otherwise from any God
> to glean a word of knowledge. But I came,
> Oedipus, who knew nothing, and I stopped her.
> I solved the riddle by my wit alone.
> Mine was no knowledge got from birds. And now
> you would expel me,
> because you think that you will find a place   400
> by Creon's throne. I think you will be sorry,

both you and your accomplice, for your plot
to drive me out. And did I not regard you
as an old man, some suffering would have taught you
that what was in your heart was treason.

Chorus

We look at this man's words and yours, my king,
and we find both have spoken them in anger.   405
We need no angry words but only thought
how we may best hit the God's meaning for us.

Teiresias

If you are king, at least I have the right
no less to speak in my defence against you.
Of that much I am master. I am no slave   410
of yours, but Loxias', and so I shall not
enroll myself with Creon for my patron.
Since you have taunted me with being blind,
here is my word for you.
You have your eyes but see not where you are
in sin, nor where you live, nor whom you live with.
Do you know who your parents are? Unknowing   415
you are an enemy to kith and kin
in death, beneath the earth, and in this life.
A deadly footed, double striking curse,
from father and mother both, shall drive you forth
out of this land, with darkness on your eyes,
that now have such straight vision. Shall there be
a place will not be harbour to your cries,   420
a corner of Cithaeron will not ring
in echo to your cries, soon, soon,—
when you shall learn the secret of your marriage,
which steered you to a haven in this house,—
haven no haven, after lucky voyage?
And of the multitude of other evils
establishing a grim equality
between you and your children, you know nothing.   425

So, muddy with contempt my words and Creon's!
Misery shall grind no man as it will you.

Oedipus

Is it endurable that I should hear
such words from him? Go and a curse go with you!   430
Quick, home with you! Out of my house at once!

Teiresias

I would not have come either had you not called me.

Oedipus

I did not know then you would talk like a fool—
or it would have been long before I called you.

Teiresias

I am a fool then, as it seems to you—   435
but to the parents who have bred you, wise.

Oedipus

What parents? Stop! Who are they of all the world?

Teiresias

This day will show your birth and will destroy you.

Oedipus

How needlessly your riddles darken everything.

Teiresias

But it's in riddle answering you are strongest.   440

Oedipus

Yes. Taunt me where you will find me great.

Teiresias

It is this very luck that has destroyed you.

Oedipus

I do not care, if it has saved this city.

Teiresias

Well, I will go. Come, boy, lead me away.

Oedipus

Yes, lead him off. So long as you are here,   445

you'll be a stumbling block and a vexation;
once gone, you will not trouble me again.

Teiresias

I have said
what I came here to say not fearing your
countenance: there is no way you can hurt me.
I tell you, king, this man, this murderer
(whom you have long declared you are in search of,
indicting him in threatening proclamation   450
as murderer of Laius)—he is here.
In name he is a stranger among citizens
but soon he will be shown to be a citizen
true native Theban, and he'll have no joy
of the discovery: blindness for sight
and beggary for riches his exchange,   455
he shall go journeying to a foreign country
tapping his way before him with a stick.
He shall be proved father and brother both
to his own children in his house; to her
that gave him birth, a son and husband both;
a fellow sower in his father's bed
with that same father that he murdered.
Go within, reckon that out, and if you find me   460
mistaken, say I have no skill in prophecy.

(*Exeunt separately Teiresias and Oedipus.*)

Chorus

Strophe

Who is the man proclaimed
by Delphi's prophetic rock
as the bloody handed murderer,   465
the doer of deeds that none dare name?
Now is the time for him to run
with a stronger foot
than Pegasus
for the child of Zeus leaps in arms upon him   470
with fire and the lightning bolt,

and terribly close on his heels
are the Fates that never miss.

Antistrophe
Lately from snowy Parnassus
clearly the voice flashed forth,
bidding each Theban track him down,   475
the unknown murderer.
In the savage forests he lurks and in
the caverns like
the mountain bull.
He is sad and lonely, and lonely his feet
that carry him far from the navel of earth;   480
but its prophecies, ever living,
flutter around his head.

Strophe
The augur has spread confusion,
terrible confusion;
I do not approve what was said   485
nor can I deny it.
I do not know what to say;
I am in a flutter of foreboding;
I never heard in the present
nor past of a quarrel between   490
the sons of Labdacus and Polybus,
that I might bring as proof
in attacking the popular fame
of Oedipus, seeking
to take vengeance for undiscovered
death in the line of Labdacus.   495

Antistrophe
Truly Zeus and Apollo are wise
and in human things all knowing;
but amongst men there is no   500
distinct judgment, between the prophet
and me—which of us is right.

One man may pass another in wisdom
but I would never agree
with those that find fault with the king
till I should see the word
proved right beyond doubt. For once
in visible form the Sphinx
came on him and all of us
saw his wisdom and in that test
he saved the city. So he will not be condemned by my mind.   512

                                        (*Enter Creon.*)

Creon

Citizens, I have come because I heard
deadly words spread about me, that the king
accuses me. I cannot take that from him.
If he believes that in these present troubles   515
he has been wronged by me in word or deed
I do not want to live on with the burden
of such a scandal on me. The report   520
injures me doubly and most vitally—
for I'll be called a traitor to my city
and traitor also to my friends and you.

Chorus

Perhaps it was a sudden gust of anger
that forced that insult from him, and no judgment.

Creon

But did he say that it was in compliance   525
with schemes of mine that the seer told him lies?

Chorus

Yes, he said that, but why, I do not know.

Creon

Were his eyes straight in his head? Was his mind right
when he accused me in this fashion?

Chorus

I do not know; I have no eyes to see   530
what princes do. Here comes the king himself.

(Enter Oedipus.)

Oedipus

    You, sir, how is it you come here? Have you so much
    brazen-faced daring that you venture in
    my house although you are proved manifestly
    the murderer of that man, and though you tried,
    openly, highway robbery of my crown?   535
    For God's sake, tell me what you saw in me,
    what cowardice or what stupidity,
    that made you lay a plot like this against me?
    Did you imagine I should not observe
    the crafty scheme that stole upon me or
    seeing it, take no means to counter it?   540
    Was it not stupid of you to make the attempt,
    to try to hunt down royal power without
    the people at your back or friends? For only
    with the people at your back or money can
    the hunt end in the capture of a crown.

Creon

    Do you know what you're doing? Will you listen
    to words to answer yours, and then pass judgment?

Oedipus

    You're quick to speak, but I am slow to grasp you,   545
    for I have found you dangerous,—and my foe.

Creon

    First of all hear what I shall say to that.

Oedipus

    At least don't tell me that you are not guilty.

Creon

    If you think obstinacy without wisdom
    a valuable possession, you are wrong.   550

Oedipus

    And you are wrong if you believe that one,
    a criminal, will not be punished only
    because he is my kinsman.

Creon

This is but just—
but tell me, then, of what offense I'm guilty?

Oedipus

Did you or did you not urge me to send   555
to this prophetic mumbler?

Creon

I did indeed,
and I shall stand by what I told you.

Oedipus

How long ago is it since Laius. . . .

Creon

What about Laius? I don't understand.

Oedipus

Vanished—died—was murdered?   560

Creon

It is long,
a long, long time to reckon.

Oedipus

Was this prophet
in the profession then?

Creon

He was, and honoured
as highly as he is today.

Oedipus

At that time did he say a word about me?

Creon

Never, at least when I was near him.   565

Oedipus

You never made a search for the dead man?

Creon

We searched, indeed, but never learned of anything.

Oedipus

Why did our wise old friend not say this then?

Creon
    I don't know; and when I know nothing, I
    usually hold my tongue.

Oedipus
                    You know this much,   570
    and can declare this much if you are loyal.

Creon
    What is it? If I know, I'll not deny it.

Oedipus
    That he would not have said that I killed Laius
    had he not met you first.

Creon
                    You know yourself
    whether he said this, but I demand that I   575
    should hear as much from you as you from me.

Oedipus
    Then hear,—I'll not be proved a murderer.

Creon
    Well, then. You're married to my sister.

Oedipus
                  Yes,
    that I am not disposed to deny.

Creon
                  You rule
    this country giving her an equal share
    in the government?

Oedipus
                  Yes, everything she wants   580
    she has from me.

Creon
                  And I, as thirdsman to you,
    am rated as the equal of you two?

Oedipus
    Yes, and it's there you've proved yourself false friend.

Creon

Not if you will reflect on it as I do.
Consider, first, if you think any one
would choose to rule and fear rather than rule   585
and sleep untroubled by a fear if power
were equal in both cases. I, at least,
I was not born with such a frantic yearning
to be a king—but to do what kings do.
And so it is with every one who has learned
wisdom and self-control. As it stands now,
the prizes are all mine—and without fear.   590
But if I were the king myself, I must
do much that went against the grain.
How should despotic rule seem sweeter to me
than painless power and an assured authority?
I am not so besotted yet that I
want other honours than those that come with profit.   595
Now every man's my pleasure; every man greets me;
now those who are your suitors fawn on me,—
success for them depends upon my favour.
Why should I let all this go to win that?
My mind would not be traitor if it's wise;   600
I am no treason lover, of my nature,
nor would I ever dare to join a plot.
Prove what I say. Go to the oracle
at Pytho and inquire about the answers,
if they are as I told you. For the rest,   605
if you discover I laid any plot
together with the seer, kill me, I say,
not only by your vote but by my own.
But do not charge me on obscure opinion
without some proof to back it. It's not just
lightly to count your knaves as honest men,   610
nor honest men as knaves. To throw away
an honest friend is, as it were, to throw
your life away, which a man loves the best.

In time you will know all with certainty;
time is the only test of honest men,
one day is space enough to know a rogue.   615

Chorus

His words are wise, king, if one fears to fall.
Those who are quick of temper are not safe.

Oedipus

When he that plots against me secretly
moves quickly, I must quickly counterplot.
If I wait taking no decisive measure   620
his business will be done, and mine be spoiled.

Creon

What do you want to do then? Banish me?

Oedipus

No, certainly; kill you, not banish you.[1]

Creon

I do not think that you've your wits about you.   626

Oedipus

For my own interests, yes.

Creon

But for mine, too,
you should think equally.

Oedipus

You are a rogue.

Creon

Suppose you do not understand?

Oedipus

But yet
I must be ruler.

1. Two lines omitted here owing to the confusion in the dialogue consequent on
the loss of a third line. The lines as they stand in Jebb's edition (1902) are:

Oed.: That you may show what manner of thing is envy.
Creon: You speak as one that will not yield or trust.
[Oed. lost line.]

Creon

Not if you rule badly.

Oedipus

O, city, city!

Creon

I too have some share   630
in the city; it is not yours alone.

Chorus

Stop, my lords! Here—and in the nick of time
I see Jocasta coming from the house;
with her help lay the quarrel that now stirs you.

(*Enter Jocasta.*)

Jocasta

For shame! Why have you raised this foolish squabbling
brawl? Are you not ashamed to air your private   635
griefs when the country's sick? Go in, you, Oedipus,
and you, too, Creon, into the house. Don't magnify
your nothing troubles.

Creon

Sister, Oedipus,
your husband, thinks he has the right to do
terrible wrongs—he has but to choose between   640
two terrors: banishing or killing me.

Oedipus

He's right, Jocasta; for I find him plotting
with knavish tricks against my person.

Creon

That God may never bless me! May I die
accursed, if I have been guilty of   645
one tittle of the charge you bring against me!

Jocasta

I beg you, Oedipus, trust him in this,
spare him for the sake of this his oath to God,
for my sake, and the sake of those who stand here.

Chorus

    Be gracious, be merciful,   649
    we beg of you.

Oedipus

    In what would you have me yield?

Chorus

    He has been no silly child in the past.
    He is strong in his oath now.
    Spare him.

Oedipus

    Do you know what you ask?

Chorus

    Yes.

Oedipus

    Tell me then.

Chorus

    He has been your friend before all men's eyes; do not cast him   656
    away dishonoured on an obscure conjecture.

Oedipus

    I would have you know that this request of yours
    really requests my death or banishment.

Chorus

    May the Sun God, king of Gods, forbid! May I die without God's   660
    blessing, without friends' help, if I had any such thought. But my
    spirit is broken by my unhappiness for my wasting country; and   665
    this would but add troubles amongst ourselves to the other
    troubles.

Oedipus

    Well, let him go then—if I must die ten times for it,   669
    or be sent out dishonoured into exile.
    It is your lips that prayed for him I pitied,
    not his; wherever he is, I shall hate him.

Creon

I see you sulk in yielding and you're dangerous
when you are out of temper; natures like yours
are justly heaviest for themselves to bear.   675

Oedipus

Leave me alone! Take yourself off, I tell you.

Creon

I'll go, you have not known me, but they have,
and they have known my innocence.

(*Exit.*)

Chorus

Won't you take him inside, lady?

Jocasta

Yes, when I've found out what was the matter.   680

Chorus

There was some misconceived suspicion of a story, and on the
other side the sting of injustice.

Jocasta

So, on both sides?

Chorus

Yes.

Jocasta

What was the story?

Chorus

I think it best, in the interests of the country, to leave it where   685
it ended.

Oedipus

You see where you have ended, straight of judgment
although you are, by softening my anger.

Chorus

Sir, I have said before and I say again—be sure that I would have   689
been proved a madman, bankrupt in sane council, if I should put
you away, you who steered the country I love safely when she

was crazed with troubles. God grant that now, too, you may   695
prove a fortunate guide for us.

Jocasta

Tell me, my lord, I beg of you, what was it
that roused your anger so?

Oedipus

Yes, I will tell you.   700
I honour you more than I honour them.
It was Creon and the plots he laid against me.

Jocasta

Tell me—if you can clearly tell the quarrel—

Oedipus

Creon says
that I'm the murderer of Laius.

Jocasta

Of his own knowledge or on information?

Oedipus

He sent this rascal prophet to me, since   705
he keeps his own mouth clean of any guilt.

Jocasta

Do not concern yourself about this matter;
listen to me and learn that human beings
have no part in the craft of prophecy.
Of that I'll show you a short proof.   710
There was an oracle once that came to Laius,—
I will not say that it was Phoebus' own,
but it was from his servants—and it told him
that it was fate that he should die a victim
at the hands of his own son, a son to be born
of Laius and me. But, see now, he,
the king, was killed by foreign highway robbers   715
at a place where three roads meet—so goes the story;
and for the son—before three days were out
after his birth King Laius pierced his ankles

and by the hands of others cast him forth
upon a pathless hillside. So Apollo   720
failed to fulfill his oracle to the son,
that he should kill his father, and to Laius
also proved false in that the thing he feared,
death at his son's hands, never came to pass.
So clear in this case were the oracles,
so clear and false. Give them no heed, I say;
what God discovers need of, easily
he shows to us himself.   725

Oedipus

                   O dear Jocasta,
as I hear this from you, there comes upon me
a wandering of the soul—I could run mad.

Jocasta

What trouble is it, that you turn again
and speak like this?

Oedipus

                  I thought I heard you say
that Laius was killed at a crossroads.   730

Jocasta

Yes, that was how the story went and still
that word goes round.

Oedipus

                 Where is this place, Jocasta,
where he was murdered?

Jocasta

                Phocis is the country
and the road splits there, one of two roads from Delphi,
another comes from Daulia.

Oedipus

                How long ago is this?   735

Jocasta

The news came to the city just before

you became king and all men's eyes looked to you.
What is it, Oedipus, that's in your mind?

Oedipus
What have you designed, O Zeus, to do with me?

Jocasta
What is the thought that troubles your heart?

Oedipus
Don't ask me yet—tell me of Laius—   740
How did he look? How old or young was he?

Jocasta
He was a tall man and his hair was grizzled
already—nearly white—and in his form
not unlike you.

Oedipus
     O God, I think I have
called curses on myself in ignorance.   745

Jocasta
What do you mean? I am terrified
when I look at you.

Oedipus
     I have a deadly fear
that the old seer had eyes. You'll show me more
if you can tell me one more thing.

Jocasta
     I will.
I'm frightened,—but if I can understand,
I'll tell you all you ask.

Oedipus
     How was his company?   750
Had he few with him when he went this journey,
or many servants, as would suit a prince?

Jocasta
In all there were but five, and among them
a herald; and one carriage for the king.

Oedipus

It's plain—its plain—who was it told you this?   755

Jocasta

The only servant that escaped safe home.

Oedipus

Is he at home now?

Jocasta

No, when he came home again
and saw you king and Laius was dead,
he came to me and touched my hand and begged   760
that I should send him to the fields to be
my shepherd and so he might see the city
as far off as he might. So I
sent him away. He was an honest man,
as slaves go, and was worthy of far more
than what he asked of me.

Oedipus

O, how I wish that he could come back quickly!   765

Jocasta

He can. Why is your heart so set on this?

Oedipus

O dear Jocasta, I am full of fears
that I have spoken far too much; and therefore
I wish to see this shepherd.

Jocasta

He will come;
but, Oedipus, I think I'm worthy too
to know what it is that disquiets you.   770

Oedipus

It shall not be kept from you, since my mind
has gone so far with its forebodings. Whom
should I confide in rather than you, who is there
of more importance to me who have passed
through such a fortune?

Polybus was my father, king of Corinth,
and Merope, the Dorian, my mother.   775
I was held greatest of the citizens
in Corinth till a curious chance befell me
as I shall tell you—curious, indeed,
but hardly worth the store I set upon it.
There was a dinner and at it a man,
a drunken man, accused me in his drink   780
of being bastard. I was furious
but held my temper under for that day.
Next day I went and taxed my parents with it;
they took the insult very ill from him,
the drunken fellow who had uttered it.
So I was comforted for their part, but   785
still this thing rankled always, for the story
crept about widely. And I went at last
to Pytho, though my parents did not know.
But Phoebus sent me home again unhonoured
in what I came to learn, but he foretold   790
other and desperate horrors to befall me,
that I was fated to lie with my mother,
and show to daylight an accursed breed
which men would not endure, and I was doomed
to be murderer of the father that begot me.
When I heard this I fled, and in the days
that followed I would measure from the stars   795
the whereabouts of Corinth—yes, I fled
to somewhere where I should not see fulfilled
the infamies told in that dreadful oracle.
And as I journeyed I came to the place
where, as you say, this king met with his death.
Jocasta, I will tell you the whole truth.   800
When I was near the branching of the crossroads,
going on foot, I was encountered by
a herald and a carriage with a man in it,
just as you tell me. He that led the way

and the old man himself wanted to thrust me   805
out of the road by force. I became angry
and struck the coachman who was pushing me.
When the old man saw this he watched his moment,
and as I passed he struck me from his carriage,
full on the head with his two pointed goad.
But he was paid in full and presently   810
my stick had struck him backwards from the car
and he rolled out of it. And then I killed them
all. If it happened there was any tie
of kinship twixt this man and Laius,
who is then now more miserable than I,   815
what man on earth so hated by the Gods,
since neither citizen nor foreigner
may welcome me at home or even greet me,
but drive me out of doors? And it is I,
I and no other have so cursed myself.   820
And I pollute the bed of him I killed
by the hands that killed him. Was I not born evil?
Am I not utterly unclean? I had to fly
and in my banishment not even see
my kindred nor set foot in my own country,
or otherwise my fate was to be yoked   825
in marriage with my mother and kill my father,
Polybus who begot me and had reared me.
Would not one rightly judge and say that on me
these things were sent by some malignant God?
O no, no, no—O holy majesty   830
of God on high, may I not see that day!
May I be gone out of men's sight before
I see the deadly taint of this disaster
come upon me.

Chorus

   Sir, we too fear these things. But until you see this man face to
   face and hear his story, hope.   835

Oedipus

Yes, I have just this much of hope—to wait until the herdsman comes.

Jocasta

And when he comes, what do you want with him?

Oedipus

I'll tell you; if I find that his story is the same as yours, I at least will be clear of this guilt.   840

Jocasta

Why what so particularly did you learn from my story?

Oedipus

You said that he spoke of highway *robbers* who killed Laius. Now if he uses the same number, it was not I who killed him. One man cannot be the same as many. But if he speaks of a man travelling   845
alone, then clearly the burden of the guilt inclines towards me.

Jocasta

Be sure, at least, that this was how he told the story. He cannot unsay it now, for every one in the city heard it—not I alone. But,   850
Oedipus, even if he diverges from what he said then, he shall never prove that the murder of Laius squares rightly with the prophecy—for Loxias declared that the king should be killed by his own son. And that poor creature did not kill him surely,—   855
for he died himself first. So as far as prophecy goes, henceforward I shall not look to the right hand or the left.

Oedipus

Right. But yet, send some one for the peasant to bring him here;   860
do not neglect it.

Jocasta

I will send quickly. Now let me go indoors. I will do nothing except what pleases you.

                                                        (*Exeunt.*)

Chorus

   Strophe
May destiny ever find me

pious in word and deed   865
prescribed by the laws that live on high:
laws begotten in the clear air of heaven,
whose only father is Olympus;
no mortal nature brought them to birth,
no forgetfulness shall lull them to sleep;   870
for God is great in them and grows not old.

Antistrophe

Insolence breeds the tyrant, insolence
if it is glutted with a surfeit, unseasonable, unprofitable,   875
climbs to the roof-top and plunges
sheer down to the ruin that must be,
and there its feet are no service.
But I pray that the God may never   880
abolish the eager ambition that profits the state.
For I shall never cease to hold the God as our protector.

Strophe

If a man walks with haughtiness
of hand or word and gives no heed   885
to Justice and the shrines of Gods
despises—may an evil doom
smite him for his ill-starred pride of heart!—
if he reaps gains without justice
and will not hold from impiety   890
and his fingers itch for untouchable things.
When such things are done, what man shall contrive
to shield his soul from the shafts of the God?
When such deeds are held in honour,   895
why should I honour the Gods in the dance?

Antistrophe

No longer to the holy place,
to the navel of earth I'll go
to worship, nor to Abae
nor to Olympia,   900
unless the oracles are proved to fit,
for all men's hands to point at.

O Zeus, if you are rightly called
the sovereign lord, all-mastering,
let this not escape you nor your ever-living power!   905
The oracles concerning Laius
are old and dim and men regard them not.
Apollo is nowhere clear in honour; God's service perishes.   910

(Enter Jocasta, carrying garlands.)

Jocasta

Princes of the land, I have had the thought to go
to the Gods' temples, bringing in my hand
garlands and gifts of incense, as you see.
For Oedipus excites himself too much
at every sort of trouble, not conjecturing,   915
like a man of sense, what will be from what was,
but he is always at the speaker's mercy,
when he speaks terrors. I can do no good
by my advice, and so I came as suppliant
to you, Lycaean Apollo, who are nearest.
These are the symbols of my prayer and this   920
my prayer: grant us escape free of the curse.
Now when we look to him we are all afraid;
he's pilot of our ship and he is frightened.

(Enter Messenger.)

Messenger

Might I learn from you, sirs, where is the house of Oedipus? Or   925
best of all, if you know, where is the king himself?

Chorus

This is his house and he is within doors. This lady is his wife and
mother of his children.

Messenger

God bless you, lady, and God bless your household! God bless   930
Oedipus' noble wife!

Jocasta

God bless you, sir, for your kind greeting! What do you want
of us that you have come here? What have you to tell us?

Messenger

Good news, lady. Good for your house and for your husband.

Jocasta

What is your news? Who sent you to us?   935

Messenger

I come from Corinth and the news I bring will give you pleasure.
Perhaps a little pain too.

Jocasta

What is this news of double meaning?

Messenger

The people of the Isthmus will choose Oedipus to be their king.   940
That is the rumour there.

Jocasta

But isn't their king still old Polybus?

Messenger

No. He is in his grave. Death has got him.

Jocasta

Is that the truth? Is Oedipus' father dead?

Messenger

May I die myself if it be otherwise!

Jocasta (to a servant)

Be quick and run to the King with the news! O oracles of the   945
Gods, where are you now? It was from this man Oedipus fled, lest
he should be his murderer! And now he is dead, in the course of
nature, and not killed by Oedipus.

(*Enter Oedipus.*)

Oedipus

Dearest Jocasta, why have you sent for me?   950

Jocasta

Listen to this man and when you hear reflect what is the outcome
of the holy oracles of the Gods.

Oedipus

Who is he? What is his message for me?

« 50 »

Jocasta

He is from Corinth and he tells us that your father Polybus is   955
dead and gone.

Oedipus

What's this you say, sir? Tell me yourself.

Messenger

Since this is the first matter you want clearly told: Polybus has
gone down to death. You may be sure of it.

Oedipus

By treachery or sickness?   960

Messenger

A small thing will put old bodies asleep.

Oedipus

So he died of sickness, it seems,—poor old man!

Messenger

Yes, and of age—the long years he had measured.

Oedipus

Ha! Ha! O dear Jocasta, why should one
look to the Pythian hearth? Why should one look   965
to the birds screaming overhead? They prophesied
that I should kill my father! But he's dead,
and hidden deep in earth, and I stand here
who never laid a hand on spear against him,—
unless perhaps he died of longing for me,
and thus I am his murderer. But they,   970
the oracles, as they stand—he's taken them
away with him, they're dead as he himself is,
and worthless.

Jocasta

                     That I told you before now.

Oedipus

You did, but I was misled by my fear.

Jocasta

Then lay no more of them to heart, not one   975

Oedipus

But surely I must fear my mother's bed?

Jocasta

Why should man fear since chance is all in all
for him, and he can clearly foreknow nothing?
Best to live lightly, as one can, unthinkingly.
As to your mother's marriage bed,—don't fear it.   980
Before this, in dreams too, as well as oracles,
many a man has lain with his own mother.
But he to whom such things are nothing bears
his life most easily.

Oedipus

All that you say would be said perfectly
if she were dead; but since she lives I must   985
still fear, although you talk so well, Jocasta.

Jocasta

Still in your father's death there's light of comfort?

Oedipus

Great light of comfort; but I fear the living.

Messenger

Who is the woman that makes you afraid?

Oedipus

Merope, old man, Polybus' wife.   990

Messenger

What about her frightens the queen and you?

Oedipus

A terrible oracle, stranger, from the Gods.

Messenger

Can it be told? Or does the sacred law
forbid another to have knowledge of it?

Oedipus

O no! Once on a time Loxias said
that I should lie with my own mother and   995

take on my hands the blood of my own father.
And so for these long years I've lived away
from Corinth; it has been to my great happiness;
but yet it's sweet to see the face of parents.

Messenger
This was the fear which drove you out of Corinth?   1000

Oedipus
Old man, I did not wish to kill my father.

Messenger
Why should I not free you from this fear, sir,
since I have come to you in all goodwill?

Oedipus
You would not find me thankless if you did.

Messenger
Why, it was just for this I brought the news,—   1005
to earn your thanks when you had come safe home.

Oedipus
No, I will never come near my parents.

Messenger
                          Son,
it's very plain you don't know what you're doing.

Oedipus
What do you mean, old man? For God's sake, tell me.

Messenger
If your homecoming is checked by fears like these.   1010

Oedipus
Yes, I'm afraid that Phoebus may prove right.

Messenger
The murder and the incest?

Oedipus
                          Yes, old man;
that is my constant terror.

Messenger

Do you know

that all your fears are empty?

Oedipus

How is that,

if they are father and mother and I their son?

Messenger

Because Polybus was no kin to you in blood.

Oedipus

What, was not Polybus my father?

Messenger

No more than I but just so much.

Oedipus

How can

my father be my father as much as one
that's nothing to me?

Messenger

Neither he nor I

begat you.

Oedipus

Why then did he call me son?

Messenger

A gift he took you from these hands of mine.

Oedipus

Did he love so much what he took from another's hand?

Messenger

His childlessness before persuaded him.

Oedipus

Was I a child you bought or found when I
was given to him?

Messenger

On Cithaeron's slopes

in the twisting thickets you were found.

Oedipus

And why
were you a traveller in those parts?

Messenger

I was
in charge of mountain flocks.

Oedipus

You were a shepherd?
A hireling vagrant?

Messenger

Yes, but at least at that time   1030
the man that saved your life, son.

Oedipus
What ailed me when you took me in your arms?

Messenger
In that your ankles should be witnesses.

Oedipus
Why do you speak of that old pain?

Messenger

I loosed you;
the tendons of your feet were pierced and fettered,—

Oedipus
My swaddling clothes brought me a rare disgrace.   1035

Messenger
So that from this you're called your present name.

Oedipus
Was this my father's doing or my mother's?
For God's sake, tell me.

Messenger

I don't know, but he
who gave you to me has more knowledge than I.

Oedipus
You yourself did not find me then? You took me
from someone else?

Messenger

Yes, from another shepherd.   1040

Oedipus

Who was he? Do you know him well enough
to tell?

Messenger

He was called Laius' man.

Oedipus

You mean the king who reigned here in the old days?

Messenger

Yes, he was that man's shepherd.

Oedipus

Is he alive   1045
still, so that I could see him?

Messenger

You who live here
would know that best.

Oedipus

Do any of you here
know of this shepherd whom he speaks about
in town or in the fields? Tell me. It's time   1050
that this was found out once for all.

Chorus

I think he is none other than the peasant
whom you have sought to see already; but
Jocasta here can tell us best of that.

Oedipus

Jocasta, do you know about this man
whom we have sent for? Is he the man he mentions?   1055

Jocasta

Why ask of whom he spoke? Don't give it heed;
nor try to keep in mind what has been said.
It will be wasted labour.

Oedipus

                          With such clues
I could not fail to bring my birth to light.

Jocasta

    I beg you—do not hunt this out—I beg you,   1060

    if you have any care for your own life.

    What I am suffering is enough.

Oedipus

                          Keep up
your heart, Jocasta. Though I'm proved a slave,
thrice slave, and though my mother is thrice slave,
you'll not be shown to be of lowly lineage.

Jocasta

    O be persuaded by me, I entreat you;

    do not do this.

Oedipus

    I will not be persuaded to let be   1065

    the chance of finding out the whole thing clearly.

Jocasta

    It is because I wish you well that I

    give you this counsel—and it's the best counsel.

Oedipus

    Then the best counsel vexes me, and has

    for some while since.

Jocasta

                          O Oedipus, God help you!

    God keep you from the knowledge of who you are!

Oedipus

    Here, some one, go and fetch the shepherd for me;

    and let her find her joy in her rich family!   1070

Jocasta

    O Oedipus, unhappy Oedipus!

    that is all I can call you, and the last thing

    that I shall ever call you.

                                              (*Exit.*)

Chorus

Why has the queen gone, Oedipus, in wild
grief rushing from us? I am afraid that trouble
will break out of this silence.

Oedipus

Break out what will! I at least shall be
willing to see my ancestry, though humble.
Perhaps she is ashamed of my low birth,
for she has all a woman's high-flown pride.
But I account myself a child of Fortune,
beneficent Fortune, and I shall not be
dishonoured. She's the mother from whom I spring;
the months, my brothers, marked me, now as small,
and now again as mighty. Such is my breeding,
and I shall never prove so false to it,
as not to find the secret of my birth.

Chorus

Strophe

If I am a prophet and wise of heart
you shall not fail, Cithaeron,
by the limitless sky, you shall not!—
to know at tomorrow's full moon
that Oedipus honours you,
as native to him and mother and nurse at once;
and that you are honoured in dancing by us, as finding favour in
sight of our king.
Apollo, to whom we cry, find these things pleasing!

Antistrophe

Who was it bore you, child? One of
the long-lived nymphs who lay with Pan—
the father who treads the hills?
Or was she a bride of Loxias, your mother? The grassy slopes
are all of them dear to him. Or perhaps Cyllene's king
or the Bacchants' God that lives on the tops

of the hills received you a gift from some
one of the Helicon Nymphs, with whom he mostly plays?

(Enter an old man, led by Oedipus' servants.)

Oedipus
 If some one like myself who never met him   1110
 may make a guess,—I think this is the herdsman,
 whom we were seeking. His old age is consonant
 with the other. And besides, the men who bring him
 I recognize as my own servants. You   1115
 perhaps may better me in knowledge since
 you've seen the man before.

Chorus
         You can be sure
 I recognize him. For if Laius
 had ever an honest shepherd, this was he.

Oedipus
 You, sir, from Corinth, I must ask you first,
 is this the man you spoke of?   1120

Messenger
        This is he
 before your eyes.

Oedipus
        Old man, look here at me
 and tell me what I ask you. Were you ever
 a servant of King Laius?

Herdsman
        I was,—
 no slave he bought but reared in his own house.

Oedipus
 What did you do as work? How did you live?

Herdsman
 Most of my life was spent among the flocks.   1125

Oedipus
 In what part of the country did you live?

Herdsman

Cithaeron and the places near to it.

Oedipus

And somewhere there perhaps you knew this man?

Herdsman

What was his occupation? Who?

Oedipus

               This man here, 1130
have you had any dealings with him?

Herdsman

           No—
not such that I can quickly call to mind.

Messenger

That is no wonder, master. But I'll make him remember what he
does not know. For I know, that he well knows the country of
Cithaeron, how he with two flocks, I with one kept company for 1135
three years—each year half a year—from spring till autumn time
and then when winter came I drove my flocks to our fold home
again and he to Laius' steadings. Well—am I right or not in what 1140
I said we did?

Herdsman

You're right—although it's a long time ago.

Messenger

Do you remember giving me a child
to bring up as my foster child?

Herdsman

             What's this?
Why do you ask this question?

Messenger

            Look old man, 1145
here he is—here's the man who was that child!

Herdsman

Death take you! Won't you hold your tongue?

Oedipus
                                No, no,
do not find fault with him, old man. Your words
are more at fault than his.

Herdsman
                              O best of masters,
how do I give offense?

Oedipus
                              When you refuse   1150
to speak about the child of whom he asks you.

Herdsman
He speaks out of his ignorance, without meaning.

Oedipus
If you'll not talk to gratify me, you
will talk with pain to urge you.

Herdsman
                              O please, sir,
don't hurt an old man, sir.

Oedipus (*to the servants*)
                              Here, one of you,
twist his hands behind him.

Herdsman
                            Why, God help me, why?   1155
What do you want to know?

Oedipus
                             You gave a child
to him,—the child he asked you of?

Herdsman
                          I did.
I wish I'd died the day I did.

Oedipus
                          You will
unless you tell me truly.

Herdsman

And I'll die

far worse if I should tell you.

Oedipus

This fellow   1160

is bent on more delays, as it would seem.

Herdsman

O no, no! I have told you that I gave it.

Oedipus

Where did you get this child from? Was it your own or did you
get it from another?

Herdsman

Not

my own at all; I had it from some one.

Oedipus

One of these citizens? or from what house?

Herdsman

O master, please—I beg you, master, please   1165

don't ask me more.

Oedipus

You're a dead man if I

ask you again.

Herdsman

It was one of the children

of Laius.

Oedipus

A slave? Or born in wedlock?

Herdsman

O God, I am on the brink of frightful speech.

Oedipus

And I of frightful hearing. But I must hear.   1170

Herdsman

The child was called his child; but she within,
your wife would tell you best how all this was.

Oedipus
  She gave it to you?

Herdsman
                    Yes, she did, my lord.

Oedipus
  To do what with it?

Herdsman
                    Make away with it.

Oedipus
  She was so hard—its mother?   1175

Herdsman
                    Aye, through fear
  of evil oracles.

Oedipus
                    Which?

Herdsman
                    They said that he
  should kill his parents.

Oedipus
                    How was it that you
  gave it away to this old man?

Herdsman
                    O master,
  I pitied it, and thought that I could send it
  off to another country and this man
  was from another country. But he saved it   1180
  for the most terrible troubles. If you are
  the man he says you are, you're bred to misery.

Oedipus
  O, O, O, they will all come,
  all come out clearly! Light of the sun, let me
  look upon you no more after today!
  I who first saw the light bred of a match
  accursed, and accursed in my living
  with them I lived with, cursed in my killing.   1185

                    (Exeunt all but the Chorus.)

Chorus

   Strophe

   O generations of men, how I
   count you as equal with those who live
   not at all!
   What man, what man on earth wins more   ·   1190
   of happiness than a seeming
   and after that turning away?
   Oedipus, you are my pattern of this,
   Oedipus, you and your fate!
   Luckless Oedipus, whom of all men
   I envy not at all.   1196

   Antistrophe

   In as much as he shot his bolt
   beyond the others and won the prize
   of happiness complete—
   O Zeus—and killed and reduced to nought
   the hooked taloned maid of the riddling speech,
   standing a tower against death for my land:
   hence he was called my king and hence
   was honoured the highest of all
   honours; and hence he ruled
   in the great city of Thebes.

   Strophe

   But now whose tale is more miserable?   1204
   Who is there lives with a savager fate?
   Whose troubles so reverse his life as his?

   O Oedipus, the famous prince
   for whom a great haven
   the same both as father and son
   sufficed for generation,
   how, O how, have the furrows ploughed
   by your father endured to bear you, poor wretch,
   and hold their peace so long?

Antistrophe

Time who sees all has found you out   1213
against your will; judges your marriage accursed,
begetter and begot at one in it.

O child of Laius,
would I had never seen you.
I weep for you and cry
a dirge of lamentation.

To speak directly, I drew my breath
from you at the first and so now I lull   1222
my mouth to sleep with your name.

                        (Enter a second messenger.)

Second Messenger

O Princes always honoured by our country,
what deeds you'll hear of and what horrors see,
what grief you'll feel, if you as true born Thebans   1225
care for the house of Labdacus's sons.
Phasis nor Ister cannot purge this house,
I think, with all their streams, such things
it hides, such evils shortly will bring forth
into the light, whether they will or not;   1230
and troubles hurt the most
when they prove self-inflicted.

Chorus

What we had known before did not fall short
of bitter groaning's worth; what's more to tell?

Second Messenger

Shortest to hear and tell—our glorious queen   1235
Jocasta's dead.

Chorus

                   Unhappy woman! How?

Second Messenger

By her own hand. The worst of what was done
you cannot know. You did not see the sight.
Yet in so far as I remember it

you'll hear the end of our unlucky queen.   1240
When she came raging into the house she went
straight to her marriage bed, tearing her hair
with both her hands, and crying upon Laius   1245
long dead—Do you remember, Laius,
that night long past which bred a child for us
to send you to your death and leave
a mother making children with her son?
And then she groaned and cursed the bed in which
she brought forth husband by her husband, children   1250
by her own child, an infamous double bond.
How after that she died I do not know,—
for Oedipus distracted us from seeing.
He burst upon us shouting and we looked
to him as he paced frantically around,
begging us always: Give me a sword, I say,   1255
to find this wife no wife, this mother's womb,
this field of double sowing whence I sprang
and where I sowed my children! As he raved
some god showed him the way—none of us there.
Bellowing terribly and led by some   1260
invisible guide he rushed on the two doors,—
wrenching the hollow bolts out of their sockets,
he charged inside. There, there, we saw his wife
hanging, the twisted rope around her neck.
When he saw her, he cried out fearfully   1265
and cut the dangling noose. Then, as she lay,
poor woman, on the ground, what happened after,
was terrible to see. He tore the brooches—
the gold chased brooches fastening her robe—
away from her and lifting them up high
dashed them on his own eyeballs, shrieking out   1270
such things as: they will never see the crime
I have committed or had done upon me!
Dark eyes, now in the days to come look on
forbidden faces, do not recognize

those whom you long for—with such imprecations
he struck his eyes again and yet again   1275
with the brooches. And the bleeding eyeballs gushed
and stained his beard—no sluggish oozing drops
but a black rain and bloody hail poured down.

So it has broken—and not on one head   1280
but troubles mixed for husband and for wife.
The fortune of the days gone by was true
good fortune—but today groans and destruction
and death and shame—of all ills can be named   1285
not one is missing.

Chorus

Is he now in any ease from pain?

Second Messenger

                    He shouts
for some one to unbar the doors and show him
to all the men of Thebes, his father's killer,
his mother's—no I cannot say the word,
it is unholy—for he'll cast himself,
out of the land, he says, and not remain   1290
to bring a curse upon his house, the curse
he called upon it in his proclamation. But
he wants for strength, aye, and some one to guide him;
his sickness is too great to bear. You, too,
will be shown that. The bolts are opening.   1295
Soon you will see a sight to waken pity
even in the horror of it.

                              (*Enter the blinded Oedipus.*)

Chorus

This is a terrible sight for men to see!
I never found a worse!
Poor wretch, what madness came upon you!   1300
What evil spirit leaped upon your life
to your ill-luck—a leap beyond man's strength!
Indeed I pity you, but I cannot

look at you, though there's much I want to ask
and much to learn and much to see.   1305
I shudder at the sight of you.

Oedipus

O, O,
where am I going? Where is my voice   1310
borne on the wind to and fro?
Spirit, how far have you sprung?

Chorus

To a terrible place whereof men's ears
may not hear, nor their eyes behold it.

Oedipus

Darkness!
Horror of darkness enfolding, resistless, unspeakable visitant sped
    by an ill wind in haste!   1315
madness and stabbing pain and memory
of evil deeds I have done!

Chorus

In such misfortunes it's no wonder
if double weighs the burden of your grief.   1320

Oedipus

My friend,
you are the only one steadfast, the only one that attends on me;
you still stay nursing the blind man.
Your care is not unnoticed. I can know   1325
your voice, although this darkness is my world.

Chorus

Doer of dreadful deeds, how did you dare
so far to do despite to your own eyes?
what spirit urged you to it?

Oedipus

It was Apollo, friends, Apollo,
that brought this bitter bitterness, my sorrows to completion.   1330
But the hand that struck me

was none but my own.
Why should I see
whose vision showed me nothing sweet to see?   1335

Chorus
    These things are as you say.

Oedipus
    What can I see to love?
    What greeting can touch my ears with joy?
    Take me away, and haste—to a place out of the way!   1340
    Take me away, my friends, the greatly miserable,
    the most accursed, whom God too hates   1345
    above all men on earth!

Chorus
    Unhappy in your mind and your misfortune,
    would I had never known you!

Oedipus
    Curse on the man who took
    the cruel bonds from off my legs, as I lay in the field.   1350
    He stole me from death and saved me,
    no kindly service.
    Had I died then
    I would not be so burdensome to friends.   1355

Chorus
    I, too, could have wished it had been so.

Oedipus
    Then I would not have come
    to kill my father and marry my mother infamously.
    Now I am godless and child of impurity,   1360
    begetter in the same seed that created my wretched self.
    If there is any ill worse than ill,   1365
    that is the lot of Oedipus.

Chorus
    I cannot say your remedy was good;
    you would be better dead than blind and living.

Oedipus

What I have done here was best done—don't tell me   1370
otherwise, do not give me further counsel.
I do not know with what eyes I could look
upon my father when I die and go
under the earth, nor yet my wretched mother—
those two to whom I have done things deserving
worse punishment than hanging. Would the sight   1375
of children, bred as mine are, gladden me?
No, not these eyes, never. And my city,
its towers and sacred places of the Gods,
of these I robbed my miserable self   1380
when I commanded all to drive *him* out,
the criminal since proved by God impure
and of the race of Laius.
To this guilt I bore witness against myself—
with what eyes shall I look upon my people?   1385
No. If there were a means to choke the fountain
of hearing I would not have stayed my hand
from locking up my miserable carcase,
seeing and hearing nothing; it is sweet   1390
to keep our thoughts out of the range of hurt.

Cithaeron, why did you receive me? why
having received me did you not kill me straight?
And so I had not shown to men my birth.

O Polybus and Corinth and the house,
the old house that I used to call my father's—   1395
what fairness you were nurse to, and what foulness
festered beneath! Now I am found to be
a sinner and a son of sinners. Crossroads,
and hidden glade, oak and the narrow way
at the crossroads, that drank my father's blood   1400
offered you by my hands, do you remember
still what I did as you looked on, and what
I did when I came here? O marriage, marriage!

you bred me and again when you had bred
bred children of your child and showed to men   1405
brides, wives and mothers and the foulest deeds
that can be in this world of ours.

Come—it's unfit to say what is unfit
to do.—I beg of you in God's name hide me   1410
somewhere outside your country, yes, or kill me,
or throw me into the sea, to be forever
out of your sight. Approach and deign to touch me
for all my wretchedness, and do not fear.
No man but I can bear my evil doom.   1415

Chorus

Here Creon comes in fit time to perform
or give advice in what you ask of us.
Creon is left sole ruler in your stead.

Oedipus

Creon! Creon! What shall I say to him?
How can I justly hope that he will trust me?   1420
In what is past I have been proved towards him
an utter liar.

(Enter Creon.)

Creon

Oedipus, I've come
not so that I might laugh at you nor taunt you
with evil of the past. But if you still
are without shame before the face of men
reverence at least the flame that gives all life,   1425
our Lord the Sun, and do not show unveiled
to him pollution such that neither land
nor holy rain nor light of day can welcome.

(To a servant.)

Be quick and take him in. It is most decent   1430
that only kin should see and hear the troubles
of kin.

Oedipus
>   I beg you, since you've torn me from
my dreadful expectations and have come
in a most noble spirit to a man
that has used you vilely—do a thing for me.
I shall speak for your own good, not for my own.

Creon
> What do you need that you would ask of me?   1435

Oedipus
> Drive me from here with all the speed you can
to where I may not hear a human voice.

Creon
> Be sure, I would have done this had not I
wished first of all to learn from the God the course
of action I should follow.

Oedipus
>   But his word   1440
has been quite clear to let the parricide,
the sinner, die.

Creon
>   Yes, that indeed was said.
But in the present need we had best discover
what we should do.

Oedipus
>   And will you ask about
a man so wretched?

Creon
>   Now even you will trust   1445
the God.

Oedipus
>   So. I command you—and will beseech you—
to her that lies inside that house give burial
as you would have it; she is yours and rightly
you will perform the rites for her. For me—

never let this my father's city have me   1450
living a dweller in it. Leave me live
in the mountains where Cithaeron is, that's called
my mountain, which my mother and my father
while they were living would have made my tomb.
So I may die by their decree who sought
indeed to kill me. Yet I know this much: 1455
no sickness and no other thing will kill me.
I would not have been saved from death if not
for some strange evil fate. Well, let my fate
go where it will.

                  Creon, you need not care   1460
about my sons; they're men and so wherever
they are, they will not lack a livelihood.
But my two girls—so sad and pitiful—
whose table never stood apart from mine,
and everything I touched they always shared—   1465
O Creon, have a thought for them! And most
I wish that you might suffer me to touch them
and sorrow with them.

      (Enter Antigone and Ismene, Oedipus' two daughters.)
O my lord! O true noble Creon! Can I   1470
really be touching them, as when I saw?
What shall I say?
Yes, I can hear them sobbing—my two darlings!
and Creon has had pity and has sent me
what I loved most?
Am I right?   1475

Creon

    You're right: it was I gave you this
because I knew from old days how you loved them
as I see now.

Oedipus

               God bless you for it, Creon,
and may God guard you better on your road
than he did me!

O children,   1480
where are you? Come here, come to my hands,
a brother's hands which turned your father's eyes,
those bright eyes you knew once, to what you see,
a father seeing nothing, knowing nothing,
begetting you from his own source of life.   1485
I weep for you—I cannot see your faces—
I weep when I think of the bitterness
there will be in your lives, how you must live
before the world. At what assemblages
of citizens will you make one? to what   1490
gay company will you go and not come home
in tears instead of sharing in the holiday?
And when you're ripe for marriage, who will he be;
the man who'll risk to take such infamy
as shall cling to my children, to bring hurt   1495
on them and those that marry with them? What
curse is not there? "Your father killed his father
and sowed the seed where he had sprung himself
and begot you out of the womb that held him."
These insults you will hear. Then who will marry you?   1500
No one, my children; clearly you are doomed
to waste away in barrenness unmarried.
Son of Menoeceus, since you are all the father
left these two girls, and we, their parents, both   1505
are dead to them—do not allow them wander
like beggars, poor and husbandless.
They are of your own blood.
And do not make them equal with myself
in wretchedness; for you can see them now
so young, so utterly alone, save for you only.
Touch my hand, noble Creon, and say yes.   1510
If you were older, children, and were wiser,
there's much advice I'd give you. But as it is,
let this be what you pray: give me a life

wherever there is opportunity
to live, and better life than was my father's.

Creon
Your tears have had enough of scope; now go within the house.   1515

Oedipus
I must obey, though bitter of heart.

Creon
In season, all is good.

Oedipus
Do you know on what conditions I obey?

Creon
                              You tell me them,
and I shall know them when I hear.

Oedipus
                         That you shall send me out
to live away from Thebes.

Creon
                    That gift you must ask of the God.

Oedipus
But I'm now hated by the Gods.

Creon
                         So quickly you'll obtain your prayer.

Oedipus
You consent then?   1520

Creon
                         What I do not mean, I do not use to say.

Oedipus
Now lead me away from here.

Creon
                         Let go the children, then, and come.

Oedipus
Do not take them from me.

Creon

> Do not seek to be master in everything,
> for the things you mastered did not follow you throughout your
> life.

> *(As Creon and Oedipus go out.)*

Chorus

> You that live in my ancestral Thebes, behold this Oedipus,—
> him who knew the famous riddles and was a man most masterful;   1525
> not a citizen who did not look with envy on his lot—
> see him now and see the breakers of misfortune swallow him!
> Look upon that last day always. Count no mortal happy till
> he has passed the final limit of his life secure from pain.   1530

OEDIPUS AT COLONUS[1]

Translated by Robert Fitzgerald

1. *Sophocles: Oedipus at Colonus*, an English Version by Robert Fitzgerald, copyright 1941, by Harcourt, Brace and Company, Inc.

CHARACTERS

Oedipus

Antigone

A Stranger

Ismene

Theseus

Creon

Polyneices

A Messenger

Chorus

OEDIPUS AT COLONUS

Long after he had left Thebes, the blinded OEDIPUS *came with* ANTIGONE
to the Attic deme of COLONUS, *where the oracle of Apollo had prophesied
that he was to die.*

SCENE: *Like the theatre, is in the open air. In the background is the grove
of the Furies at Colonus in Attica, about a mile northwest of
Athens. A statue or stele of Colonus, a legendary horseman and
hero, can be seen stage left. Stage right, a flat rock jutting out
among the trees of the grove. Downstage, center, another ridge of
rock.*

TIME: *Early afternoon of a day about twenty years after the action of
King Oedipus.*

SCENE I

(*Oedipus, old, blind, bearded and ragged, but carrying
himself well, enters stage right, led by Antigone.*)

Oedipus
 My daughter—daughter of the blind old man—
 Where, I wonder, have we come to now?
 What place is this, Antigone? What people?
 Who will be kind to Oedipus this evening
 And give the wanderer charity?

 Though he ask little and receive still less,   5
 It is sufficient:
       Suffering and time,
 Vast time, have been instructors in contentment,
 Which kingliness teaches too.
        But now, child,
 If you can see a place where we might rest,
 Some public place or consecrated park,   10
 Let me stop and sit down there.
 And then let us inquire where we may be.

As foreigners and strangers we must learn
From the local people, and do as they direct.

Antigone

Father, poor tired Oedipus, the towers
That crown the city still seem far away;   15
As for this place, it is clearly a holy one,
Shady with vines and olive trees and laurel;
Snug in their wings within, the nightingales
Make a sweet music.
                         Rest on this rough stone.
It was a long road for an old man to travel.   20

Oedipus

Help me sit down; take care of the blind man.

Antigone

After so long, you need not tell me, father.

Oedipus

And now have you any idea where we are?

Antigone

This place I do not know; the city is Athens.

Oedipus

Yes, everyone we met has told us that.   25

Antigone

Then shall I go and ask?

Oedipus

Do, child, if there is any life near-by.

Antigone

Oh, but indeed there is; I need not leave you;
I see a man, now, not far away from us.

Oedipus

Is he coming this way? Has he started towards us?   30

                        (*The Stranger enters, left.*)

Antigone

Here he is now.

Say what seems best to you,
Father; the man is here.

Oedipus
Friend, my daughter's eyes serve for my own.
She tells me we are fortunate enough to meet you,
And no doubt you will inform us—   35

Stranger
Do not go on;
First move from where you sit; the place is holy;
It is forbidden to walk upon that ground.

Oedipus
What ground is this? What god is honored here?

Stranger
It is not to be touched, no one may live upon it;
Most dreadful are its divinities, most feared,
Daughters of darkness and mysterious earth.   40

Oedipus
Under what solemn name shall I invoke them?

Stranger
The people here prefer to address them as Gentle
All-seeing Ones; elsewhere there are other names.

Oedipus
Then may they be gentle to the suppliant.
For I shall never leave this resting place.   45

Stranger
What is the meaning of this?

Oedipus
It was ordained;
I recognize it now.

Stranger
Without authority
From the city government I dare not move you;
First I must show them what it is you are doing.

Oedipus

Friend, in the name of God, bear with me now!
I turn to you for light; answer the wanderer.   50

Stranger

Speak. You will not find me discourteous.

Oedipus

What is this region into which I've come?

Stranger

Whatever I can tell you, I will tell.
This country, all of it, is blessed ground;
The god of the sea loves it; in it the firecarrier   55
Prometheus has his influence; in particular
That spot you rest on has been called this earth's
Doorsill of Brass, and buttress of great Athens.
All men of this land claim descent from him
Whose statue stands near-by: Colonus the horseman,
And bear his name in common with their own.   60
That is this country, stranger: honored less
In histories than in the hearts of the people.

Oedipus

Then people live in the land?

Stranger

                                    Yes, certainly,
The clan of those descended from that hero.   65

Oedipus

Ruled by a king? Or do the people rule?

Stranger

The land is governed from Athens, by Athens' king.

Oedipus

And who is he whose word has power here?

Stranger

Theseus, son of Aegeus, the king before him.

Oedipus

Ah. Would someone then go to this king for me?   70

Stranger
To tell him what? Perhaps to urge his coming?

Oedipus
To tell him a small favor will gain him much.

Stranger
What service can a blind man render him?

Oedipus
All I shall say will be clear-sighted indeed.

Stranger
Listen, stranger: I wish you no injury;   75
You seem well-born, though obviously unlucky;
Stay where you are, exactly where I found you,
And I'll inform the people of what you say—
Not in the town, but here—it rests with them
To decide if you should stay or must move on.   80

(Exit Stranger, left.)

Oedipus
Child, has he gone?

Antigone
Yes, father. Now you may speak tranquilly,
For only I am with you.

Oedipus (praying)
                    Ladies whose eyes
Are terrible: Spirits: upon your sacred ground
I have first bent my knees in this new land;   85
Therefore be mindful of me and of Apollo,
For when he gave me oracles of evil,
He also spoke of this:
                    A resting place,
After long years, in the last country, where
I should find home among the sacred Furies: 90
That there I might round out my bitter life,
Conferring benefit on those who received me,
A curse on those who have driven me away.

Portents, he said, would make me sure of this:
Earthquake, thunder, or God's smiling lightning; 95
But I am sure of it now, sure that you guided me
With feathery influence upon this road,
And led me here into your hallowed wood.

How otherwise could I, in my wandering,
Have sat down first with you in all this land, 100
I who drink not, with you who love not wine?

How otherwise had I found this chair of stone?
Grant me then, goddesses, passage from life at last,
And consummation, as the unearthly voice foretold;
Unless indeed I seem not worth your grace:
Slave as I am to such unending pain 105
As no man had before.

                                    O hear my prayer,
Sweet children of original Darkness! Hear me,
Athens, city named for great Athena,
Honored above all cities in the world!
Pity a man's poor carcase and his ghost,
For Oedipus is not the strength he was. 110

Antigone

Be still. Some elderly men are coming this way,
Looking for the place where you are seated.

Oedipus

I shall be still. You get me clear of the path,
And hide me in the wood, so I may hear
What they are saying. If we know their temper 115
We shall be better able to act with prudence.

                    (*Oedipus and Antigone withdraw into the grove.*)

CHORAL DIALOGUE

(*The Chorus enters from the left. Here, and throughout the
play, its lines may be taken by various members as
seems suitable.*)

Chorus

Look for him. Who could he be? Where
Is he? Where is the stranger
Impious, blasphemous, shameless!   120
Use your eyes, search him out!
Cover the ground and uncover him!
                    Vagabond!
The old man must be a vagabond,
Not of our land, for he'd never   125
Otherwise dare to go in there,
In the inviolate thicket
Of those whom it's futile to fight,
Those whom we tremble to name.
When we pass we avert our eyes—
                    Close our eyes!—   130
In silence, without conversation,
Shaping our prayers with our lips.
But now, if the story is credible,
Some alien fool has profaned it;
Yet I have looked over all the grove and   135
                    Still cannot see him;
Cannot say where he has hidden.

                    (*Oedipus comes forward from the wood.*)

Oedipus

That stranger is I. As they say of the blind,
Sounds are the things I see.

Chorus

                    Ah!   140
His face is dreadful! His voice is dreadful!

Oedipus

Do not regard me, please, as a law-breaker.

Chorus

Zeus defend us, who is this old man?

Oedipus

One whose fate is not quite to be envied,

O my masters, and men of this land;   145
That must be evident: why, otherwise,
               Should I need this girl
To lead me, her frailty to put my weight on?

Chorus

Ah! His eyes are blind!   150
And were you brought into the world so?
Unhappy life—and so long!
Well, not if I can help it,
Will you have this curse besides.—
               Stranger! you   155
Trespass there! But beyond there,
In the glade where the grass is still,
Where the honeyed libations drip
In the rill from the brimming spring,
You must not step! O stranger,   160
It is well to be careful about it!
               Most careful!
Stand aside and come down then!
There is too much space between us!
Say, wanderer, can you hear?   165
If you have a mind to tell us
Your business, or wish to converse with our council,
               Come down from that place!
Only speak where it's proper to do so!

Oedipus

Now, daughter, what is the way of wisdom?   170

Antigone

We must do just as they do here, father;
We should give in now, and listen to them.

Oedipus

Stretch out your hand to me.

Antigone

               There, I am near you.

Oedipus

Sirs, let there be no injustice done me,
Once I have trusted you, and left my refuge.   175

> (*Led by Antigone, he starts downstage.*)

Chorus

Never, never, will anyone drive you away
From rest in this land, old man!

Oedipus

Shall I come further?

Chorus

Yes, further.

Oedipus

And now?

Chorus

You must guide him, girl;   180
You can see how much further to come.

Antigone

Come with your blind step, father;
This way; come where I lead you.

Chorus

Though the land is strange, newcomer,
You've weathered much; take heart;   185
What the state has long held hateful,
Hate, and respect what it loves.

Oedipus

Lead me on, then, child,
To where we may speak or listen respectfully;   190
Let us not fight necessity.

Chorus

Now! Go no further than that platform there,
Formed of the natural rock.

Oedipus

This?

Chorus

Far enough; you can hear us.

Oedipus
Shall I sit down?

Chorus

Yes, sit there   195
To the left on the ridge of the rock.

Antigone
Father, this is where I can help you;
You must keep step with me; gently now.

Oedipus
Ah, me!

Antigone
Lean your old body on my arm;   200
It is I who love you; let yourself down.

Oedipus
How bitter blindness is!

(*He is seated on the rock downstage, center.*)

Chorus
Now that you are at rest, poor man,
Tell us, what is your name?
Who are you, wanderer?   205
What is the land of your ancestors?

Oedipus
I am an exile, friends; but do not ask me . . .

Chorus
What is it you fear to say, old man?

Oedipus
No, no, no! Do not go on   210
Questioning me! Do not ask my name!

Chorus
Why not?

Oedipus
My star was unspeakable.

Chorus
Speak!

Oedipus
My child, what can I say to them?

Chorus
Answer us, stranger; what is your race,
Who was your father? 215

Oedipus
God help me, what will become of me, child?

Antigone
Tell them; there is no other way.

Oedipus
Well, then, I will; I cannot hide it.

Chorus
Between you, you greatly delay. Speak up!

Oedipus
Have you heard of Laius' family?

Chorus
Ah! 220

Oedipus
Of the race of Labdacidae?

Chorus
Ah, Zeus!

Oedipus
And ruined Oedipus?

Chorus
You are he!

Oedipus
Do not take fright from what I say—

Chorus
Oh, dreadful!

Oedipus
> I am accursed.

Chorus
> Oh, fearful!

Oedipus
> Antigone, what will happen now?   225

Chorus
> Away with you! Out with you! Leave our country!

Oedipus
> And what of the promises you made me?

Chorus
> God will not punish the man
> Who makes return for an injury:
> Deceivers may be deceived: 230
> They play a game that ends
> In grief, and not in pleasure.
> Leave this grove at once!
> Our country is not for you!
> Wind no further   235
> Your clinging evil upon us!

Antigone
> O men of reverent mind!
> Since you will not suffer my father,
> Old man though he is,
> And though you know his story—
> He never knew what he did—   240
> Take pity still on my unhappiness,
> And let me intercede with you for him.
> Not with lost eyes, but looking in your eyes
> As if I were a child of yours, I beg   245
> Mercy for him, the beaten man! O hear me!
> We are thrown upon your mercy as on God's;
> > Be kinder than you seem!
> By all you have and own that is dear to you:
> Children, wives, possessions, gods, I pray you!   250

For you will never see in all the world
   A man whom God has led
   Escape his destiny!

SCENE 2

Chorus

  Child of Oedipus, indeed we pity you,
  Just as we pity him for his misfortune;   255
  But we tremble to think of what the gods may do;
  We could not dare to speak more generously!

Oedipus

  What use is reputation then? What good
  Comes of a noble name? A noble fiction!
  For Athens, so they say, excels in piety;   260
  Has power to save the wretched of other lands;
  Can give them refuge; is unique in this.
  Yet, when it comes to me, where is her refuge?
  You pluck me from these rocks and cast me out,
  All for fear of a name!
        Or do you dread   265
  My strength? my actions? I think not, for I
  Suffered those deeds more than I acted them,
  As I might show if it were fitting here
  To tell my father's and my mother's story . . .
  For which you fear me, as I know too well.

  And yet, how was I evil in myself?   270
  I had been wronged, I retaliated; even had I
  Known what I was doing, was that evil?
  Then, knowing nothing, I went on. Went on.
  But those who wronged me knew, and ruined me.

  Therefore I beg of you before the gods,   275
  For the same cause that made you move me—
  In reverence of your gods—give me this shelter,
  And thus accord those powers what is theirs.
  Think: their eyes are fixed upon the just,

Fixed on the unjust, too; no impious man   280
Can twist away from them forever.
Now, in their presence, do not blot your city's
Luster by bending to unholy action;
As you would receive an honest petitioner,
Give me, too, sanctuary; though my face   285
Be dreadful in its look, yet honor me!

For I come here as one endowed with grace
By those who are over Nature; and I bring
Advantage to this race, as you may learn
More fully when some lord of yours is here.   290
Meanwhile be careful to be just.

Chorus

Old man,
This argument of yours compels our wonder.
It was not feebly worded. I am content
That higher authorities should judge this matter.   295

Oedipus

And where is he who rules the land, strangers?

Chorus

In his father's city; but the messenger
Who sent us here has gone to fetch him also.

Oedipus

Do you think a blind man will so interest him
As to bring him such a distance?   300

Chorus

I do, indeed, when he has heard your name.

Oedipus

But who will tell him that?

Chorus

It is a long road, and the rumors of travellers
Have a way of wandering. He will have word of them;
Take heart—he will be here. Old man, your name   305

Has gone over all the earth; though he may be
At rest when the news comes, he will come quickly.

Oedipus

Then may he come with luck for his own city,
As well as for me. . . . The good befriend themselves.

Antigone

O Zeus! What shall I say? How interpret this?   310

Oedipus

Antigone, my dear child, what is it?

Antigone

A woman
Riding a Sicilian pony and coming towards us;
She is wearing the wide Thessalian sun-hat;
I don't know!   315
Is it or isn't it? Or am I dreaming?
I think so; yes!—No. I can't be sure. . . .

Ah, poor child,
It is no one else but she! And she is smiling   320
Now as she comes! It is my dear Ismene!

Oedipus

What did you say, child?

                    (*Ismene enters, with one Attendant.*)

Antigone

That I see your daughter!
My sister! Now you can tell her by her voice.

Ismene

O father and sister together! Dearest voices!
Now I have found you—how, I scarcely know—   325
I don't know how I shall see you through my tears!

Oedipus

Child, you have come?

Ismene

Father, how old you seem!

Oedipus
Child, are you here?

Ismene
                              And such a time I had!

Oedipus
Touch me, little one.

Ismene
                              I shall hold you both!

Oedipus
My children . . . and sisters.

Ismene
                              Oh, unhappy people!   330

Oedipus
She and I?

Ismene
                              And I with you, unhappy.

Oedipus
But, child, why have you come?

Ismene
                              For your sake, father.

Oedipus
You missed me?

Ismene
                              Yes; and I have news for you.
I came with the one person I could trust.

Oedipus
Why, where are your brothers? Could they not do it?   335

Ismene
They are—where they are. It is a hard time for them.

Oedipus
Ah! They behave as if they were Egyptians,
Bred the Egyptian way! Down there, the men
Sit indoors all day long, weaving;
The women go out and attend to business.   340
Just so your brothers, who should have done this work

Sit by the fire like home-loving girls,
And you two, in their place, must bear my hardships.

One, since her childhood ended and her body
Gained its power, has wandered ever with me,   345
An old man's governess; often in the wild
Forest going without shoes, and hungry,
Beaten by many rains, tired by the sun;   350
Yet she rejected the sweet life of home
So that her father should have sustenance.

And you, my daughter, once before came out,
Unknown to Thebes, bringing me news of all
The oracle had said concerning me;   355
And you remained my faithful outpost there,
When I was driven from that land.
                              But now,
What news, Ismene, do you bring your father?
Why have you left your house to make this journey?
You came for no light reason, I know that;
It must be something serious for me.   360

Ismene

I will pass over the troubles I have had
Searching for your whereabouts, father.
They were hard enough to bear; and I will not
Go through it all again in telling of them.
In any case, it is your sons' troubles   365
That I have come to tell you.
First it was their desire, as it was Creon's,
That the throne should pass to him; that thus the city
Should be defiled no longer: such was their reasoning
When they considered our people's ancient curse
And how it enthralled your pitiful family.   370
But then some fury put it in their hearts—
O pitiful again!—to itch for power:
For seizure of prerogative and throne;
And it was the younger and the less mature

Who stripped his elder brother, Polyneices,   375
Of place and kingship, and then banished him.

But now the people hear he has gone to Argos,
Into the valley land, has joined that nation,
And is enlisting friends among its warriors,
Telling them Argos shall honorably win   380
Thebes and her plain, or else eternal glory.
This is not a mere recital, father;
But terrible truth!
                           How long will it be, I wonder,
Before the gods take pity on your distress?

Oedipus

You have some hope then that they are concerned   385
With my deliverance?

Ismene

                           I have, father.
The latest sentences of the oracle . . .

Oedipus

How are they worded? What do they prophesy?

Ismene

That you shall be much solicited by our people
Before your death—and after—for their welfare.   390

Oedipus

And what could anyone hope from such as I?

Ismene

The oracles declare their strength's in you—

Oedipus

When I am finished, I suppose I am strong!

Ismene

For the gods who threw you down sustain you now.

Oedipus

Slight favor, now I am old! My doom was early.   395

Ismene

    The proof of it is that Creon is coming to you
    For that same reason, and soon: not by and by.

Oedipus

    To do what, daughter? Tell me about this.

Ismene

    To settle you near the land of Thebes, and so
    Have you at hand; but you may not cross the border.   400

Oedipus

    What good am I to them outside the country?

Ismene

    It is merely that if your burial were unlucky,
    That would be perilous for them.

Oedipus

                Ah, then!
    No god's assistance is needed in comprehending.

Ismene

    Therefore they want to keep you somewhere near,
    Just at the border, where you'll not be free.   405

Oedipus

    And will they compose my shade with Theban dust?

Ismene

    Ah, father! No. Your father's blood forbids it.

Oedipus

    Then they shall never hold me in their power!

Ismene

    If so, some day it will be bitter for them.

Oedipus

    How will that be, my child?

Ismene

              When they shall stand   410
    Where you are buried, and feel your anger there.

Oedipus

What you have said—from whom did you hear it, child?

Ismene

The envoys told me when they returned from Delphi.

Oedipus

Then all this about me was spoken there?

Ismene

According to those men, just come to Thebes.   415

Oedipus

Has either of my sons had word of this?

Ismene

They both have, and they understand it well.

Oedipus

The scoundrels! So they knew all this, and yet
Would not give up the throne to have me back?

Ismene

It hurts me to hear it, but I can't deny it.   420

Oedipus

Gods!
Put not their fires of ambition out!
Let the last word be mine upon this battle
They are about to join, with the spears lifting!
I'd see that the one who holds the sceptre now   425
Would not have power long, nor would the other,
The banished one, return!

                        These were the two
Who saw me in disgrace and banishment
And never lifted a hand for me. They heard me
Howled from the country, heard the thing proclaimed!   430

And will they say I wanted exile then,
An appropriate clemency, granted by the state?
That is all false! The truth is that at first

My mind was a boiling caldron; nothing so sweet
As death, death by stoning, could have been given me;   435
Yet no one there would grant me that desire.
It was only later, when my madness cooled,
And I had begun to think my rage excessive,
My punishment too great for what I had done;
Then it was that the city—in its good time!—   440
Decided to be harsh, and drove me out.
They could have helped me then; they could have
Helped him who begot them! Would they do it?
For lack of a little word from that fine pair
Out I went, like a beggar, to wander forever!   445
Only by grace of these two girls, unaided,
Have I got food or shelter or devotion;
The others held their father of less worth
Than sitting on a throne and being king.

Well, they shall never win me in their fight!   450
Nor will they profit from the rule of Thebes.
I am sure of that; I have heard the prophecies
Brought by this girl; I think they fit those others
Spoken so long ago, and now fulfilled.
So let Creon be sent to find me: Creon,   455
Or any other of influence in the state.
If you men here consent—as do those powers
Holy and awful, the spirits of this place—
To give me refuge, then shall this city have
A great savior; and woe to my enemies!   460

Chorus
    Oedipus: you are surely worth our pity:
    You, and your children, too. And since you claim
    Also to be a savior of our land,
    I'd like to give you counsel for good luck.

Oedipus
    Dear friend! I'll do whatever you advise.   465

Chorus

    Make expiation to these divinities
    Whose ground you violated when you came.

Oedipus

    In what way shall I do so? Tell me, friends.

Chorus

    First you must bring libations from the spring
    That runs forever; and bring them with clean hands.   470

Oedipus

    And when I have that holy water, then?

Chorus

    There are some bowls there, by a skillful potter;
    Put chaplets round the brims, over the handles.

Oedipus

    Of myrtle springs, or woolen stuff, or what?

Chorus

    Take the fleeces cropped from a young lamb.   475

Oedipus

    Just so; then how must I perform the rite?

Chorus

    Facing the quarter of the morning light,
    Pour your libations out.

Oedipus

    Am I to pour them from the bowls you speak of?

Chorus

    In three streams, yes; the last one, empty it.

Oedipus

    With what should it be filled? Tell me this, too.   480

Chorus

    With water and honey; but with no wine added.

Oedipus

And when the leaf-dark earth receives it?

Chorus

Lay three times nine young shoots of olive on it
With both your hands; meanwhile repeat this prayer:

Oedipus

This I am eager to hear: it has great power.   485

Chorus

That as we call them Eumenides,
Which means the gentle of heart,
May they accept with gentleness
The suppliant and his wish.

So you, or he who prays for you, address them;

But do not speak aloud or raise a cry;
Then come away, and do not turn again.   490
If you will do all this, I shall take heart
And stand up for you; otherwise, O stranger,
I should be seriously afraid for you.

Oedipus

Children, you hear the words of these good people?

Antigone

Yes; now tell us what we ought to do.

Oedipus

It need not be performed by me; I'm far   495
From having the strength or sight for it—I have neither.
Let one of you go and carry out the ritual.
One soul, I think, often can make atonement
For many others, if it be sincere.
Now do it quickly.—Yet do not leave me alone!   500
I could not move without the help of someone.

Ismene

I'll go and do it. But where am I to go?
Where shall I find the holy place, I wonder?

Chorus

    On the other side of the wood, girl. If you need it,   505
    You may get help from the attendant there.

Ismene

    I am going now. Antigone, you'll stay
    And care for father. Even if it were hard,
    I should not think it so, since it is for him.

       (Ismene goes out, right. The chorus draws nearer to Oedipus.)

CHORAL DIALOGUE

Chorus

    What evil things have slept since long ago   510
      It is not sweet to awaken;
      And yet I long to be told—

Oedipus

                What?

Chorus

    Of that heartbreak for which there was no help,
      The pain you have had to suffer.

Oedipus

    For kindness' sake, do not open   515
      My old wound, and my shame.

Chorus

    It is told everywhere, and never dies;
    I only want to hear it truly told.

Oedipus

    Ah! Ah!

Chorus

             Consent I beg you;
    Give me my wish, and I shall give you yours.   520

Oedipus

    I had to face a thing most terrible,
      Not willed by me, I swear;
      I would have abhorred it all.

Chorus

So?

Oedipus

Though I did not know, Thebes married me to evil;   525
    Fate and I were joined there.

Chorus

    Then it was indeed your mother
    With whom the thing was done?

Oedipus

    Ah! It is worse than death to have to hear it!
    Strangers! Yes: and these two girls of mine . . .   530

Chorus

    Go on—

Oedipus

                        These luckless two
    Were given birth by her who gave birth to me.

Chorus

    These then are daughters; they are also—

Oedipus

    Sisters: yes, their father's sisters . . .   535

Chorus

    Ah, pity!

Oedipus

                        Pity, indeed. What throngs
    Of pities come into my mind!

Chorus

    You suffered—

Oedipus

                        Yes, unspeakably.

Chorus

    You sinned—

Oedipus

            No, I did not sin!

Chorus

How not?

Oedipus

I thought
Of her as my reward. Ah, would I had never won it!   550
Would I had never served the State that day!

Chorus

Unhappy man—and you also killed—

Oedipus

What is it now? What are you after?

Chorus

Killed your father!

Oedipus

God in heaven!
You strike again where I am hurt.

Chorus

You killed him.

Oedipus

Killed him. Yet, there is—   545

Chorus

What more?

Oedipus

A just extenuation.
This:
I did not know him; and he wished to murder me.
Before the law—before God—I am innocent!

(The Chorus turns at the approach of Theseus.)

SCENE 3

Chorus

The king is coming! Aegeus' eldest son,
Theseus: news of you has brought him here.   550

(Theseus enters with soldiers, left.)

« 104 »

Theseus

    In the old time I often heard men tell
    Of the bloody extinction of your eyes.
    Even if on my way I were not informed,
    I'd recognize you, son of Laius.
    The garments and the tortured face   555
    Make plain your identity. I am sorry for you.
    And I should like to know what favor here
    You hope for from the city and from me:
    Both you and your unfortunate companion.
    Tell me. It would be something dire indeed   560
    To make me leave you comfortless; for I
    Too was an exile. I grew up abroad,
    And in strange lands I fought as few men have
    With danger and with death.
    Therefore no wanderer shall come, as you do,   565
    And be denied my audience or aid.
    I know I am only a man; I have no more
    To hope for in the end than you have.

Oedipus

    Theseus, in those few words your nobility
    Is plain to me. I need not speak at length;   570
    You have named me and my father accurately,
    Spoken with knowledge of my land and exile.
    There is, then, nothing left for me to tell
    But my desire; and then the tale is ended.

Theseus

    Tell me your wish, then; let me hear it now.   575

Oedipus

    I come to give you something, and the gift
    Is my own beaten self: no feast for the eyes;
    Yet in me is a more lasting grace than beauty.

Theseus

    What grace is this you say you bring to us?

Oedipus

In time you'll learn, but not immediately.   580

Theseus

How long, then, must we wait to be enlightened?

Oedipus

Until I am dead, and you have buried me.

Theseus

Your wish is burial? What of your life meanwhile?
Have you forgotten that?—or do you care?

Oedipus

It is all implicated in my burial.   585

Theseus

But this is a brief favor you ask of me.

Oedipus

See to it, nevertheless! It is not simple.

Theseus

You mean I shall have trouble with your sons?

Oedipus

Those people want to take me back there now.

Theseus

Will you not go? Is exile admirable?   590

Oedipus

No. When I would have returned, they would not have it.

Theseus

What childishness! You are surely in no position—

Oedipus

When you know me, rebuke me; not till then!

Theseus

Well, tell me more. I must not speak in ignorance.

Oedipus

Theseus, I have been wounded more than once.   595

Theseus
> Is it your family's curse that you refer to?

Oedipus
> Not merely that; for all Greece buzzes with it.

Theseus
> Then what is the wound that is so pitiless?

Oedipus
> Think how it is with me. I was expelled
> From my own land by my own sons; and now,   600
> As a parricide, my return is not allowed.

Theseus
> How can they summon you, if this is so?

Oedipus
> The sacred oracle compels them to.

Theseus
> They fear some punishment from his forebodings?

Oedipus
> They fear they will be struck down in this land!   605

Theseus
> And how could war arise between these nations?

Oedipus
> Most gentle son of Aegeus! The immortal
> Gods alone have neither age nor death!
> All other things almighty Time disquiets.
> Earth wastes away; the body wastes away;   610
> Faith dies; distrust is born.
> And imperceptibly the spirit changes
> Between a man and his friend, or between two cities.
> For some men soon, for others in later time,
> Their pleasure sickens; or love comes again.   615
> And so with you and Thebes: the sweet season
> Holds between you now; but time goes on,
> Unmeasured Time, fathering numberless

Nights, unnumbered days: and on one day
They'll break apart with spears this harmony— 620
All for a trivial word.
And then my sleeping and long-hidden corpse,
Cold in the earth, will drink hot blood of theirs,
If Zeus endures; if his son's word is true . . .

However: there's no felicity in speaking
Of hidden things. Let me come back to this: 625
Be careful that you keep your word to me;
For if you do you'll never say of Oedipus
That he was given refuge uselessly—
Or if you say it, then the gods have lied.

Chorus

My lord: before you came this man gave promise
Of having power to make his words come true. 630

Theseus

Who would reject his friendship? Is he not
One who would have, in any case, an ally's
Right to our hospitality?
Moreover he has asked grace of our deities,
And offers no small favor in return. 635
As I value that favor, I shall not refuse
This man's desire; I declare him a citizen.

And if it should please our friend to remain here,
I direct you to take care of him;
Or else he may come with me.
                                    Whatever you choose,
Oedipus, we shall be happy to accord. 640
You know your own needs best; I accede to them.

Oedipus

May God bless men like these!

Theseus

What do you say then? Shall it be my house?

Oedipus
If it were right for me. But the place is here . . .

Theseus
And what will you do here?—Not that I oppose you.   645

Oedipus
Here I shall prevail over those who banished me.

Theseus
Your presence, as you say, is a great blessing.

Oedipus
If you are firm in doing what you promise.

Theseus
You can be sure of me; I'll not betray you.

Oedipus
I'll not ask pledges, as I would of scoundrels.   650

Theseus
You'd get no more assurance than by my word.

Oedipus
I wonder how you will behave?

Theseus
                                You fear?

Oedipus
That men will come—

Theseus
                                These men will attend to them.

Oedipus
Look: when you leave me—

Theseus
                                I know what to do!

Oedipus
I am oppressed by fear!

Theseus
                                I feel no fear.   655

Oedipus

You do not know the menace!

Theseus

I do know

No man is going to take you against my will.
Angry men are liberal with threats
And bluster generally. When the mind
Is master of itself, threats are no matter.   660
These people may have dared to talk quite fiercely
Of taking you; perhaps, as I rather think,
They'll find a sea of troubles in the way.
Therefore I should advise you to take heart.
Even aside from me and my intentions,
Did not Apollo send and guide you here?   665
However it may be, I can assure you,
While I'm away, my name will be your shield.

(*Exit Theseus and soldiers. The Chorus turns to the audience.*)

CHORAL POEM

Chorus

The land beloved of horsemen, fair
Colonus takes a guest;
He shall not seek another home,   670
For this, in all the earth and air,
Is most secure and loveliest.

In the god's untrodden vale
Where leaves and berries throng,
And wine-dark ivy climbs the bough,
The sweet, sojourning nightingale
Murmurs all day long.   675

No sun nor wind may enter there
Nor the winter's rain;
But eve through the shadow goes
Dionysus reveler,
Immortal maenads in his train.   680

Here with drops of heaven's dews
At daybreak all the year,
The clusters of narcissus bloom,
Time-hallowed garlands for the brows
Of those great ladies whom we fear.   685

The crocus like a little sun
Blooms with its yellow ray;
The river's fountains are awake,
And his nomadic streams that run
Unthinned forever, and never stay;   690

But like perpetual lovers move
On the maternal land.
And here the choiring Muses come,
And the divinity of love
With the gold reins in her hand.

*(The Chorus may now shift its grouping or otherwise
indicate a change of theme.)*

Chorus
And our land has a thing unknown
On Asia's sounding coast   695
Or in the sea-surrounded west
Where Agamemnon's race has sway:
The olive, fertile and self-sown,
The terror of our enemies
That no hand tames nor tears away—
The blessed tree that never dies!—
But it will mock the swordsman in his rage.

Ah, how it flourishes in every field,
Most beautifully here!   700
The gray-leafed tree, the children's nourisher!
No young man nor one partnered by his age
Knows how to root it out nor make
Barren its yield;
For Zeus the Father smiles on it with sage

Eyes that forever are awake,   705
And Pallas watches with her sea-pale eyes.

Last and grandest praise I sing
To Athens, nurse of men,
For her great pride and for the splendor
Destiny has conferred on her.   710
Land from which fine horses spring!
Land where foals are beautiful!
Land of the sea and the sea-farer!
Upon whose lovely littoral
The god of the sea moves, the son of Time.

That lover of our land I praise again,
Who found our horsemen fit
For first bestowal of the curb and bit,   715
To discipline the stallion in his prime;
And strokes to which our oarsmen sing,
Well-fitted, oak and men,
Whose long sea-oars in wondrous rhyme
Flash from the salt foam, following
The hundred-footed sea-wind and the gull.

*(At the conclusion of this, Antigone is standing stage
right, looking off-stage attentively.)*

SCENE 4

Antigone
Land so well spoken of and praised so much!   720
Now is the time to show those words are true.

Oedipus
What now, my child?

Antigone (returning to him)
                              A man is coming towards us,
And it is Creon—not unaccompanied, father.

Oedipus
Most kindly friends! I hope you may give proof,
And soon, of your ability to protect me!   725

Chorus

Don't be afraid: you'll see. I may be old,
But the nation's strength has not grown old.

(*Enter Creon, right, with guards.*)

Creon

Gentlemen, and citizens of this land:
I can see from your eyes that my arrival
Has been a cause of sudden fear to you;   730
Do not be fearful. And say nothing hostile!
I have not come for any hostile action,
For I am old, and know this city has
Power, if any city in Hellas has.

But for this man here: I, despite my age,   735
Am sent to bring him to the land of Thebes.
This is not one man's mission, but was ordered
By the whole Theban people. I am their emissary
Because it fell to me as a relative
To mourn his troubles more than anyone.

So, now, poor Oedipus, come home.   740
You have heard my message. The people of the city
Are right in summoning you—I most of all,
For most of all, unless I am worst of men,
I grieve for your unhappiness, old man.
I see you ravaged as you are, a stranger   745
Everywhere, never at rest,
With only a girl to serve you in your need.—
I never thought she'd fall to such indignity,
Poor child! And yet she has;   750
Forever tending you, leading a beggar's
Life with you; a grown-up girl who knows
Nothing of marriage; whoever comes can take her. . . .

Is not this a disgrace? I weep to see it!
Disgrace for you, for me, for all our people!
We cannot hide what is so palpable,   755
But you, if you will listen to me, Oedipus—

And in the name of your father's gods, listen!—
Bury the whole thing now; agree with me
To go back to your city and your home!

Take friendly leave of Athens, for she deserves it;
But you should have more reverence for Thebes,
Since long ago she was your kindly nurse.   760

Oedipus

You brazen rascal! Playing your rascal's tricks
In righteous speeches, as you always would!
Why do you try it? How can you think to take me
Into that snare I should so hate if taken?

That time when I was sick with my private   765
Agony: when I would lightly have left the earth—
You had no mind to give me what I wanted!
But when at long last I had had my fill
Of rage and grief, and in my quiet house
Began to find some comfort: that was the time
You chose to rout me out.   770
How precious was this kinship to you then?
It is the same thing now: you see this city
And all its people being kind to me,
So you attempt to coax me away from them!
A cruel thing, for all your soothing words.

What pleasure is there in being amiable   775
To those who do not want your amiability?

Suppose that when you wanted something terribly
A man should neither grant it you nor give
Sympathy even; but later when you were glutted
With all your heart's desire, should give it then,
When charity was no charity at all?
Would you not think the kindness somewhat hollow?   780
That is the sort of kindness you offer me:
Generous in words, but in reality evil.

Now I will tell these men, and prove you evil.
You come to take me, but not to take me home;
Rather to settle me outside the city
So that the city may escape my curse, 785
Escape from punishment by Athens.
                    Yes;
But you'll not have it. What you'll have is this:
My vengeance active in that land forever;
And what my sons will have of my old kingdom
Is just so much room as they need to die in! 790

Now who knows better the destiny of Thebes?
I do, for I have had the best informants:
Apollo, and Zeus himself who is his father.
And yet you come here with your fraudulent speech
All whetted up! The more you talk, the more 795
Harm, not good, you'll get by it!—
However, I know you'll never believe that.—

Only leave us! Let us live here in peace!
Is it a bad life, if it gives us pleasure?

Creon
    Which of us do you consider is more injured 800
    By talk like this? You hurt only yourself.

Oedipus
    I am perfectly content, so long as you
    Can neither wheedle me nor fool these others.

Creon
    Unhappy man! Shall it be plain that time
    Brings you no wisdom? that you shame your age? 805

Oedipus
    What repartee! I know no honest man
    Able to speak so well under all conditions!

Creon
    To speak much is one thing; to speak to the point's another!

Oedipus

As if you spoke so little but so fittingly!

Creon

No, not fittingly for a mind like yours!   810

Oedipus

Go away! I speak for these men also!
Stop busybodying here where I must live!

Creon

I call on these—not you!—as witnesses
Of what rejoinder you have made to friends.—
If I ever take you—

Oedipus

                            With these men fighting for me,
Who is going to take me by violence?   815

Creon

You'll have pain enough without that, I promise you!

Oedipus

What are you up to? What is behind that brag?

Creon

Your two daughters: one of them I have just now
Had seized and carried off, and I'll take this one!

Oedipus

Ah!

Creon

            You'll soon have better reason to groan about it!   820

Oedipus

You have my child?

Creon

                            And this one in a moment!

Oedipus

Ah, friends! What will you do? Will you betray me?
Are you not going to drive this thief away?

Chorus
    Go, stranger! Off with you! You have no right
    To do what you are doing, or what you have done!   825

Creon (to Guards)
    You there: it would be well to take her now,
    Whether she wants to go with you or not.

                            (*Two Guards approach Antigone.*)

Antigone
    Oh, God, where shall I run? What help is there
    From gods or men?

Chorus
                            What are you doing, stranger?

Creon
    I will not touch this man; only her who is mine.   830

Oedipus
    O masters of this land!

Chorus
                            This is unjust!

Creon
    No, just!

Chorus
            Why so?

Creon
                    I take what belongs to me!

Oedipus
    O Athens!

                            (*The Guards pinion Antigone's arms.*)

Chorus
    What are you doing, stranger? Will you
    Let her go? Must we have a test of strength?   835

Creon
    Hold off!

Chorus
                    Not while you persist in doing this!

Creon
Your city will have war if you hurt me!

Oedipus
Did I not proclaim this?

Chorus (to Guards)
      Take your hands
Off the child at once!

Creon
      What you cannot enforce,
Do not command!

Chorus
I tell you, let go!

Creon
       And I tell you—on your way!   840

    (*The Guards pull Antigone toward the right.*)

Chorus
Help! Here, men of Colonus! Help! Help!
The city, my city, is pillaged!
Hurry! Help, ho!

Antigone
They drag me away. How wretched! O friends, friends!

Oedipus (groping)
Where are you, child?

Antigone
      They have overpowered me!   845

Oedipus
Give me your hands, little one!

Antigone
      I cannot do it!

Creon (to Guards)
Will you get on with her?

        (*They go out, right.*)

Oedipus
    God help me now!

Creon
    With these two sticks at any rate you'll never
    Guide yourself again! But since you wish
    To conquer your own people—by whose command,   850
    Though I am royal, I have performed this act—
    Go on and conquer! Later, I think, you'll learn
    That now as before you have done yourself no good
    By gratifying your temper against your friends!
    Anger has always been your greatest sin!   855

Chorus (approaching Creon)
    Control yourself, stranger!

Creon
    Don't touch me, I say!

Chorus
    I'll not release you! Those two girls were stolen!

Creon
    By God, I'll have more booty in a moment
    To bring my city! I'll not stop with them!

Chorus
    Now what are you about?

Creon
                I'll take him, too!   860

Chorus
    A terrible thing to say!

Creon
                It will be done!

Chorus
    Not if the ruler of our land can help it!

Oedipus
    Voice of shamelessness! Will you touch me?

Creon
    Silence, I say!

Oedipus
                    No! May the powers here
Not make me silent until I say this curse: 865
You scoundrel, who have cruelly taken her
Who served my naked eyepits as their eyes!
On you and yours forever may the sun god,
Watcher of all the world, confer such days
As I have had, and such an age as mine!   870

Creon
Do you see this, citizens of this country?

Oedipus
They see both me and you; and they see also
That when I am hurt I have only words to avenge it!

Creon
I'll not stand for it longer! Alone as I am,
And slow with age, I'll try my strength to take him!   875

                    (*Creon goes slowly toward Oedipus.*)
Oedipus
Ah!

Chorus
                    You are a bold man, friend,
If you think you can do this!

Creon
                    I do think so!
Chorus
If you could do it, our city would be finished!

Creon
In a just cause the weak will beat the strong!   880

Oedipus
You hear his talk?

Chorus
                    By Zeus, he shall not do it!
Creon
Zeus may determine that, but you will not.

Chorus

Is this not criminal!

Creon (laying hold of Oedipus)

If so, you'll bear it!

Chorus

Ho, everyone! Captains, ho!

Hurry up! Come on the run!   885

They are well on their way by now!

                    (*Theseus enters, left, with armed men.*)

Theseus

Why do you shout? What is the matter here?

Of what are you afraid?

You have interrupted me as I was sacrificing

To the great god of the sea, Colonus's patron.

Tell me everything, so I may know;

I do not care to make such haste for nothing.   890

Oedipus

O dearest friend—I recognize your voice—

A despicable thing has just been done to me!

Theseus

What is it? Who is the man who did it? Tell me.

Oedipus

This Creon has had my daughters bound and stolen.   895

Theseus

What's that you say?

Oedipus

                    Yes; now you know my loss.

Theseus (to his men)

One of you go on the double

To the altar place and rouse the people there;

Make them leave the sacrifice at once

And run full speed, both foot and cavalry

As hard as they can gallop, for the place   900

Where the two highways come together.

The girls must not be permitted to pass there,
Or I will be a laughing-stock to this fellow,
As if I were a man to be handled roughly!
Go on, do as I tell you! Quick!

(Exit Soldier, left.)

This fellow—

If I should act in anger, as he deserves,   905
I wouldn't let him go without chastisement;
But he shall be subject to the sort of laws
He has himself imported here.—

(To Creon)

You: you shall never leave this land of Attica
Until you produce those girls here in my presence;   910
For your behavior is an affront to me,
A shame to your own people and your nation.

You come to a city-state that practices justice,
A state that rules by law, and by law only;
And yet you cast aside her authority,   915
Take what you please, and worse, by violence,
As if you thought there were no men among us,
Or only slaves; and as if I were nobody.

I doubt that Thebes is responsible for you:
She has no propensity for breeding rascals.   920
And Thebes would not applaud you if she knew
You tried to trick me and to rob the gods
By dragging helpless people from their sanctuary!

Were I a visitor in your country—
No matter how immaculate my claims—   925
Without consent from him who ruled the land,
Whoever he might be, I'd take nothing.
I think I have some notion of the conduct
Proper to one who visits a friendly city.
You bring disgrace upon an honorable
Land—your own land, too; a long life   930
Seems to have left you witless as you are old.

I said it once and say it now again:
Someone had better bring those girls here quickly,
Unless you wish to prolong your stay with us
Under close guard, and not much liking it.   935
This is not just a speech; I mean it, friend.

Chorus

Now do you see where you stand? Thebes is just,
But you are adjudged to have acted wickedly.

Creon

It was not that I thought this state unmanly,
Son of Aegeus; nor ill-governed, either;   940
Rather I did this thing in the opinion
That no one here would love my citizens
So tenderly as to keep them against my will . . .
And surely, I thought, no one would give welcome
To an unholy man, a parricide,   945
A man with whom his mother had been found!
Such at least was my estimate of the wisdom
Native to the Areopagus; I thought
Athens was not a home for such exiles.
In that belief I considered him my prize.   950
Even so, I'd not have touched him had he not
Called down curses on my race and me;
That was an injury that deserved reprisal.
There is no old age for a man's anger,
Only death; the dead cannot be hurt.   955

You'll do whatever you wish in this affair,
For even though my case is right and just,
I am weak, without support. Nevertheless,
Old as I am, I'll try to hold you answerable.

Oedipus

O arrogance unashamed! Whose age do you   960
Think you are insulting, mine or yours?
The bloody deaths, the incest, the calamities
You speak so glibly of: I suffered them,

By fate, against my will! It was God's pleasure,
And perhaps our race had angered him long ago.   965
In me myself you could not find such evil
As would have made me sin against my own.
And tell me this: if there were prophecies
Repeated by the oracles of the gods,
That father's death should come through his own son,   970
How could you justly blame it upon me?
On me, who was yet unborn, yet unconceived,
Not yet existent for my father and mother?
If then I came into the world—as I did come—
In wretchedness, and met my father in fight,   975
And knocked him down, not knowing that I killed him
Nor whom I killed—again, how could you find
Guilt in that unmeditated act?
As for my mother—damn you, you have no shame,
Though you are her own brother, in forcing me   980
To speak of that unspeakable marriage;
But I shall speak, I'll not be silent now
After you've let your foul talk go so far!
Yes, she gave me birth—incredible fate!—
But neither of us knew the truth; and she
Bore my children also—and then her shame.
But one thing I do know: you are content   985
To slander her as well as me for that;
While I would not have married her willingly
Nor willingly would I ever speak of it.

No: I shall not be judged an evil man,
Neither in that marriage nor in that death
Which you forever charge me with so bitterly.—   990
Just answer me one thing:
If someone tried to kill you here and now,
You righteous gentleman, what would you do,
Inquire first if the stranger was your father?
Or would you not first try to defend yourself?

I think that since you like to be alive 995
You'd treat him as the threat required; not
Look around for assurance that you were right.
Well, that was the sort of danger I was in,
Forced into it by the gods. My father's soul,
Were it on earth, I know would bear me out.

You, however, being a knave—and since you 1000
Think it fair to say anything you choose,
And speak of what should not be spoken of—
Accuse me of all this before these people.
You also think it clever to flatter Theseus,
And Athens—her exemplary government;
But in your flattery you have forgotten this: 1005
If any country comprehends the honors
Due to the gods, this country knows them best;
Yet you would steal me from Athens in my age
And in my time of prayer; indeed, you seized me,
And you have taken and carried off my daughters.

Now for that profanation I make my prayer, 1010
Calling on the divinities of the grove
That they shall give me aid and fight for me;
So you may know what men defend this town.

Chorus
My lord, our friend is worthy; he has had
Disastrous fortune; yet he deserves our comfort. 1015

Theseus
Enough of speeches. While the perpetrators
Flee, we who were injured loiter here.

Creon
What will you have me do?—since I am worthless.

Theseus
You lead us on the way. You can be my escort.
If you are holding the children in this neighborhood 1020
You yourself will uncover them to me.

If your retainers have taken them in flight,
The chase is not ours; others are after them.
And they will never have cause to thank their gods
For getting free out of this country.
All right. Move on. And remember that the captor   1025
Is now the captive; the hunter is in the snare.
What was won by stealth will not be kept.

In this you'll not have others to assist you;
And I know well you had them, for you'd never
Dare to go so far in your insolence   1030
Were you without sufficient accomplices.
You must have had a reason for your confidence,
And I must reckon with it. The whole city
Must not seem overpowered by one man.
Do you understand at all? Or do you think
That what I say is still without importance?   1035

Creon
    To what you say I make no objection here.
    At home we, too, shall determine what to do.

Theseus
    If you must threaten, do so on the way.
    Oedipus, you stay here, and rest assured
    That unless I perish first I'll not draw breath   1040
    Until I put your children in your hands.

Oedipus
    Bless you for your noble heart, Theseus!
    And good luck to you in what you do for us!

            (*Two Soldiers take Creon by the arms and march him out,*
                right, followed by Theseus and the rest of his men.
                    The Chorus follows a short way and stands
                        gazing after them.)

                        CHORAL POEM
Chorus
    Ah, God, to be where the pillagers make stand!
    To hear the shout and brazen sound of war!   1045

Or maybe on Apollo's sacred strand,
Or by that torchlit Eleusinian shore

Where pilgrims come, whose lips the golden key   1050
Of sweet-voiced ministers has rendered still,
To cherish there with grave Persephone
Consummate rest from death and mortal ill;

For even to those shades the warrior king   1055
Will press the fighting on—until he take
The virgin sisters from the foemen's ring,
Within his country, for his country's sake!

It may be they will get beyond the plain
And reach the snowy mountain's western side,   1060
If their light chariots have the racing rein,
If they have ponies, and if they can ride;

Yet they'll be taken: for the god they fear
Fights for our land, and Theseus sends forth   1065
His breakneck cavalry with all its gear
Flashing like mountain lightning to the north.

These are the riders of Athens, conquered never;
They honor her whose glory all men know,
And honor the god of the sea, who loves forever   1070
The feminine earth that bore him long ago.

> (*A shift of grouping, and the four following stanzas
> taken each by a separate voice.*)

Chorus

Has the fight begun? May it begin!
The presentiment enchants my mind   1075
That they shall soon give in!
And free the daughters of the blind
From hurt by their own kind!

For God will see some noble thing
Before this day is over.

Forevisioning the fight, and proud,   1080
Would I could be a soaring dove

And circle the tall cloud;
So might I gaze down from above
On the mêlée I love.

For God will see some noble thing
Before this day is over.

All highest of immortals! Hail,   1085
Great Zeus who see all things below!
Let not our troopers fail;
But give them luck to snare and throw
And bring the quarry low!

And you shall see some noble thing
Before this day is over.

Stern Pallas, hear us! Apollo, hear!   1090
Hunter and sister who give chase
To the swift and dappled deer:
Be our protectors! Lend your grace
To our land and our race!

And you shall see some noble thing
Before this day is over.

> (*There is a long pause, and then the Chorus turns*
> *to Oedipus in joy.*)

SCENE 5

Chorus

O wanderer! You will not say I lied;
I who kept lookout for you!
I see them now—the two girls—here they come
With our armed men around them!

Oedipus

Ah, where? Do you really mean it?

> (*Theseus comes in leading by the hand Antigone and*
> *Ismene, followed by Soldiers.*)

Antigone

Father, father!

I wish some god would give you eyes to see   1100
The noble prince who brings us back to you!

Oedipus

Ah, child! You are really here?

Antigone

Yes, for the strength

Of Theseus and his kind followers saved us.

Oedipus

Come to your father, child, and let me touch you
Whom I had thought never to touch again!   1105

Antigone

It shall be as you ask; I wish it as much as you.

Oedipus

Where are you?

Antigone

We are coming to you together.

Oedipus

My sweet children!

Antigone

To our father, sweet indeed.

Oedipus

My staff and my support!

Antigone

And partners in sorrow.

Oedipus

I have what is dearest to me in the world.   1110
To die, now, would not be so terrible,
Since you are near me.

Press close to me, child,

Be rooted in your father's arms; rest now
From the cruel separation, the going and coming;
And tell me the story as briefly as you can: 1115
A little talk is enough for girls so tired.

Antigone

    Theseus saved us: he is the one to tell you;
    Neither you nor I had much to do with it!

Oedipus

    Dear friend: don't be offended if I continue
    To talk to these two children overlong;   1120
    I had scarce thought they would be seen again!
    Be sure I understand that you alone
    Made this joy possible for me.
    You are the one that saved them, no one else.
    And may the gods give you such destiny
    As I desire for you: and for your country.   1125
    For I have found you truly reverent,
    Decent, and straight in speech: you only
    Of all mankind.
    I know it, and I thank you with these words.
    All that I have I owe to your courtesy;—
    Now give me your right hand, my lord,   1130
    And if it be permitted, let me kiss you. . . .

    What am I saying? How can a wretch like me
    Desire to touch a man who has no stain
    Of evil in him? No, no; I will not do it;
    And neither shall you touch me. The only ones   1135
    Fit to be fellow suffers of mine
    Are those with such experience as I have.
    Receive my salutation where you are.
    And for the rest, be kindly to me still
    As you have been up to now.

Theseus

    That you should talk a long time to your children
    In joy at seeing them—why, that's no wonder!   1140
    Or that you should address them before me—
    There's no offense in that. It is not in words
    That I should wish my life to be distinguished,
    But rather in things done.

Have I not shown that? I was not a liar   1145
In what I swore I'd do for you, old man.

I am here; and I have brought them back
Alive and safe, for all they were threatened with.
As to how I found them, how I took them, why
Brag of it? You will surely learn from them.

However, there is a matter that just now   1150
Came to my attention on my way here—
A trivial thing to speak of, and yet puzzling;
I want your opinion on it.
It is best for a man not to neglect such things.

Oedipus

What is it, son of Aegeus? Tell me,
So I may know on what you desire counsel.   1155

Theseus

They say some man is here who claims to be
A relative of yours, though not of Thebes;
For some reason he has thrown himself in prayer
Before Poseidon's altar, where I was making
Sacrifice before I came.

Oedipus

What is his country? What is he praying for?   1160

Theseus

All I know is this: he asks, they tell me,
A brief interview with you, and nothing more.

Oedipus

What about, I wonder?
It can't be a slight matter, if he is praying.

Theseus

They say he only asks to speak to you
And then to depart safely by the same road.   1165

Oedipus

Who could it be who would come here to pray?

Theseus

    Think: have you any relative in Argos
    Who might desire this favor of you?

Oedipus

                   Dear friend!
    Say no more!

Theseus

                What is the matter with you?

Oedipus

    No more!

Theseus

                   But: what is the matter? Tell me.   1170

Oedipus

    When I heard "Argos" I knew the petitioner.

Theseus

    And who is he whom I must prepare to dislike?

Oedipus

    A son of mine, my lord, and a hated one.
    Nothing could be more painful than to listen to him.

Theseus

    But why? Is it not possible to listen   1175
    Without doing anything you need not do?
    Why should it annoy you so to hear him?

Oedipus

    My lord, even his voice is hateful to me.
    Don't beat me down; don't make me yield in this!

Theseus

    But now consider if you are not obliged
    To do so by his supplication here:
    Perhaps you have a duty to the god.   1180

Antigone

    Father: listen to me, even if I am young.
    Allow this man to satisfy his conscience
    And give the gods whatever he thinks their due.
    And let our brother come here, for my sake.

Don't be afraid: he will not throw you off   1185
In your resolve, nor speak offensively.
What is the harm in hearing what he says?
If he has ill intentions, he'll betray them.
You sired him; even had he wronged you, father,
And wronged you impiously, still you could not   1190
Rightfully wrong him in return!
Do let him come!
      Other men have bad sons,
And other men are swift to anger; yet
They will accept advice, they will be swayed
By their friends' pleading, even against their nature.
Reflect, not on the present, but on the past;   1195
Think of your mother's and your father's fate
And what you suffered through them! If you do,
I think you'll see how terrible an end
Terrible wrath may have.
You have, I think, a permanent reminder
In your lost, irrecoverable eyes. . . .   1200
Ah, yield to us! If our request is just,
We need not, surely, be importunate;
And you, to whom I have not yet been hard,
Should not be obdurate with me!

Oedipus

Child, your talk wins you a pleasure
That will be pain for me. If you have set   1205
Your heart on it, so be it.

Only, Theseus: if he is to come here,
Let no one have power over my life!

Theseus

That is the sort of thing I need hear only
Once, not twice, old man. I do not boast,
But you should know your life is safe while mine is.   1210

   (Theseus goes out, left, with his Soldiers, leaving two on
     guard. The Chorus turns to address the audience.)

CHORAL POEM

Chorus

Though he has watched a decent age pass by,
A man will sometimes still desire the world.
I swear I see no wisdom in that man.
The endless hours pile up a drift of pain
More unrelieved each day; and as for pleasure,   1215
When he is sunken in excessive age,
You will not see his pleasure anywhere.
The last attendant is the same for all,
Old men and young alike, as in its season   1220
Man's heritage of underworld appears:
There being then no epithalamion,
No music and no dance. Death is the finish.

Not to be born surpasses thought and speech.
The second best is to have seen the light   1225
And then to go back quickly whence we came.
The feathery follies of his youth once over,   1230
What trouble is beyond the range of man?
What heavy burden will he not endure?
Jealousy, faction, quarreling, and battle—
The bloodiness of war, the grief of war.
And in the end he comes to strengthless age,   1235
Abhorred by all men, without company,
Unfriended in that uttermost twilight
Where he must live with every bitter thing.

This is the truth, not for me only,
But for this blind and ruined man.
Think of some shore in the north the   1240
Concussive waves make stream
This way and that in the gales of winter:
It is like that with him:
The wild wrack breaking over him
From head to foot, and coming on forever;
Now from the plunging down of the sun,   1245

Now from the sunrise quarter,
Now from where the noonday gleams,
Now from the night and the north.

(Antigone and Ismene have been looking off-stage, left.
Antigone turns.)

SCENE 6

Antigone

I think I see the stranger near us now,
And no men with him, father; but his eyes   1250
Swollen with weeping as he comes.

(Polyneices enters, left.)

Oedipus

Who comes?

Antigone

The one whom we have had so long in mind;
It is he who stands here; it is Polyneices.

Polyneices

Ah, now what shall I do? Sisters, shall I
Weep for my misfortunes or for those   1255
I see in the old man, my father,
Whom I have found here in an alien land,
With you two girls, an outcast for so long,
And with such garments! The abominable
Filth grown old with him, rotting his sides!
And on his sightless face the ragged hair   1260
Streams in the wind. There's the same quality
In the food he carries for his thin old belly.
All this I learn too late.
And I swear now that I have been villainous   1265
In not supporting you! You need not wait
To hear it said by others!

Only, think:
Compassion limits even the power of God;
So may there be a limit for you, father!

For all that has gone wrong may still be healed,
And surely the worst is over!   1270

Why are you silent?
Speak to me, father! Don't turn away from me!
Will you not answer me at all? Will you
Send me away without a word?
                              Not even
Tell me why you are enraged against me?

Daughters of Oedipus, my own sisters,   1275
Try to move your so implacable father;
Do not let him reject me in such contempt!
Make him reply!
                         I am here on pilgrimage. . . .

Antigone
   Poor brother: you yourself must tell him why.   1280
   As men speak on they may sometimes give pleasure,
   Sometimes annoy, or sometimes touch the heart;
   And so somehow provide the mute with voices.

Polyneices
   I will speak out then; your advice is fair.
   First, however, I must claim the help   1285
   Of that same god, Poseidon, from whose altars
   The governor of this land has lifted me
   And sent me here, giving me leave to speak
   And to await response, and a safe passage.
   These are the favors I desire from you,
   Stranger, and from my sisters and my father.   1290

   And now, father, I will tell you why I came.
   I am a fugitive, driven from my country,
   Because I thought fit, as the eldest born,
   To take my seat upon your sovereign throne.
   For that, Eteocles, the younger of us,   1295
   Banished me—but not by a decision
   In argument or ability or arms;
   Merely because he won the city over.

Of this I believe the Furies that pursue you
Were indeed the cause: and so I hear   1300
From clairvoyants whom I afterwards consulted. . . .

Then, when I went into the Dorian land,
I took Adrastus as my father-in-law,
And bound to me by oath whatever men
Were known as leaders or as fighters there;
My purpose being to form an expedition
Of seven troops of spearmen against Thebes.—   1305
With which enlistment may I die for justice
Or else expel the men who exiled me!

So it is. Then why should I come here now?
Father, my prayers must be made to you!
Mine and those of all who fight with me!   1310
Their seven columns under seven captains
Even now complete the encirclement of Thebes:
Men like Amphiareus, the hard spear thrower,
Expert in spears and in the ways of eagles;
Second is Tydeus, the Aetolian,   1315
Son of Oeneus; third is Eteoclus,
Born in Argos; fourth is Hippomedon
(His father, Talaus, sent him); Capaneus,
The fifth, has sworn he'll raze the town of Thebes
With fire-brands; and sixth is Parthenopaeus,   1320
An Arcadian who roused himself to war—
Son of that virgin famous in the old time
Who long years afterward conceived and bore him—
Parthenopaeus, Atalanta's son.
And it is I, your son—or if I am not
Truly your son, since evil fathered me,
At least I am called your son—it is I who lead
The fearless troops of Argos against Thebes.   1325

Now in the name of these two children, father,
And for your own soul's sake, we all implore
And beg you to give up your heavy wrath

Against me! I go forth to punish him,
The brother who robbed me of my fatherland!   1330
If we can put any trust in oracles,
They say that those you bless shall come to power.

Now by the gods and fountains of our people,
I pray you, listen and comply! Are we not beggars
Both of us, and exiles, you and I?   1335
We live by paying court to other men;
The same fate follows us.
But as for him—how insupportable!—
He lords it in our house, luxuriates there,
Laughs at us both!

If you will stand by me in my resolve,
I'll waste no time or trouble whipping him;   1340
And then I'll re-establish you at home,
And settle there myself, and throw him out.
If your will is the same as mine, it's possible
To promise this. If not, I can't be saved.   1345

Chorus
    For the sake of the one who sent him, Oedipus,
    Speak to this man before you send him back.

Oedipus
    Yes, gentlemen: but were it not Theseus,
    The sovereign of your land, who sent him here,   1350
    Thinking it right that he should have an answer,
    You never would have heard a sound from me.

    Well: he has asked, and he shall hear from me
    A kind of answer that will not overjoy him.
    You scoundrel!
                        When it was you who held
    Throne and authority—as your brother now   1355
    Holds them in Thebes—you drove me into exile:
    Me, your own father: made me a homeless man,
    Insuring me these rags you blubber over

When you behold them now—now that you, too,
Have fallen on evil days and are in exile.

Weeping is no good now. However long   1360
My life may last, I have to see it through;
But I regard you as a murderer!
For you reduced me to this misery,
You made me an alien. Because of you
I have begged my daily bread from other men.
If I had not these children to sustain me,   1365
I might have lived or died for all your interest.
But they have saved me, they are my support,
And are not girls, but men, in faithfulness.
As for you two, you are no sons of mine!

And so it is that there are eyes that watch you   1370
Even now; though not as they shall watch
If those troops are in fact marching on Thebes.
You cannot take that city. You'll go down
All bloody, and your brother, too.
                    For I
Have placed that curse upon you before this,   1375
And now I invoke that curse to fight for me,
That you may see a reason to respect
Your parents, though your birth was as it was;
And though I am blind, not to dishonor me.
These girls did not.

And so your supplication and your throne   1380
Are overmastered surely,—if accepted
Justice still has place in the laws of God.
Now go! For I abominate and disown you!
You utter scoundrel! Go with the malediction
I here pronounce for you: that you shall never   1385
Master your native land by force of arms,
Nor ever see your home again in Argos,
The land below the hills; but you shall die
By your own brother's hand, and you shall kill

The brother who banished you. For this I pray.
And I cry out to the hated underworld   1390
That it may take you home; cry out to those
Powers indwelling here; and to that Power
Of furious War that filled your hearts with hate!

Now you have heard me. Go: tell it to Thebes,
Tell all the Thebans; tell your faithful fighting
Friends what sort of honors   1395
Oedipus has divided among his sons!

Chorus

Polyneices, your coming here has given me
No joy at all. Now go away at once.

Polyneices

Ah, what a journey! What a failure!
My poor companions! See the finish now   1400
Of all we marched from Argos for! See me . . .
For I can neither speak of this to anyone
Among my friends, nor lead them back again;
I must go silently to meet this doom.

O sisters—daughters of his, sisters of mine!   1405
You heard the hard curse of our father:
For God's sweet sake, if father's curse comes true,
And if you find some way to return home,
Do not, at least, dishonor me in death!
But give me a grave and what will quiet me.   1410
Then you shall have, besides the praise he now
Gives you for serving him, an equal praise
For offices you shall have paid my ghost.

Antigone

Polyneices, I beseech you, listen to me!

Polyneices

Dearest—what is it? Tell me, Antigone.   1415

Antigone
>Withdraw your troops to Argos as soon as you can.
>Do not go to your own death and your city's!

Polyneices
>But that is impossible. How could I command
>That army, even backward, once I faltered?

Antigone
>Now why, boy, must your anger rise again?   1420
>What is the good of laying waste your homeland?

Polyneices
>It is shameful to run; and it is also shameful
>To be a laughing-stock to a younger brother.

Antigone
>But see how you fulfill his prophecies!
>Did he not cry that you should kill each other?   1425

Polyneices
>He wishes that. But I cannot give way.

Antigone
>Ah, I am desolate! But who will dare
>Go with you, after hearing the prophecies?

Polyneices
>I'll not report this trifle. A good commander
>Tells what is encouraging, not what is not.   1430

Antigone
>Then you have made up your mind to this, my brother?

Polyneices
>Yes. And do not try to hold me back.
>The dark road is before me; I must take it,
>Doomed by my father and his avenging Furies.
>God bless you if you do what I have asked: 1435
>It is only in death that you can help me now.
>Now let me go. Good-bye! You will not ever
>Look in my eyes again.

Antigone

You break my heart!

Polyneices

Do not grieve for me.

Antigone

Who would not grieve for you,
Sweet brother! You go with open eyes to death!   1440

Polyneices

Death, if that must be.

Antigone

No! Do as I ask!

Polyneices

You ask the impossible.

Antigone

Then I am lost,
If I must be deprived of you!

Polyneices

All that
Rests with the powers that are over us,—
Whether it must be so or otherwise.
You two—I pray no evil comes to you,   1445
For all men know you merit no more pain.

*(Polyneices goes out, left. There is a dead silence;
then the Chorus meditates.)*

Choral Poem and Dialogue

Chorus

So in this new event we see
New forms of terror working through the blind,
Or else inscrutable destiny.   1450
I am not one to say "This is in vain"
Of anything allotted to mankind.
Though some must fall, or fall to rise again,
Time watches all things steadily—   1455

(A terrific peal of thunder.)

Ah, Zeus! Heaven's height has cracked!

(Thunder and lightning.)

Oedipus

O my child, my child! Could someone here—
Could someone bring the hero, Theseus?

Antigone

Father, what is your reason for calling him?

Oedipus

God's beating thunder, any moment now,   1460
Will clap me underground: send for him quickly!

(Thunder and lightning.)

Chorus

Hear it cascading down the air!
The god-thrown, the gigantic, holy sound!
Terror crawls to the tips of my hair!   1465
My heart shakes!
          There the lightning flames again!
What heavenly marvel is it bringing 'round?
I fear it, for it never comes in vain,
But for man's luck or his despair. . . .   1470

(Another terrific peal.)

Ah, Zeus! Majestic heaven!

Oedipus

My children, the appointed end has come;
I can no longer turn away from it.

Antigone

How do you know? What is the sign that tells you?

Oedipus

I know it clearly now. Let someone quickly   1475
Send for the king and bring him here to me!

(Thunder and lightning.)

Chorus

Hear the wild thunder fall!
Towering Nature is transfixed!

Be merciful, great spirit, if you run   1480
This sword of darkness through our mother land;
Come not for our confusion,
And deal no blows to me,
Though your tireless Furies stand
By him whom I have looked upon.
Great Zeus, I make my prayer to thee!   1485

Oedipus

Is the king near by? Will he come in time
To find me still alive, my mind still clear?

Antigone

Tell me what it is you have in mind!

Oedipus

To give him now, in return for his great kindness,
The blessing that I promised I would give.   1490

                                        (*Thunder.*)

Chorus

O noble son, return!
No matter if you still descend
In the deep fastness of the sea god's grove,
To make pure offering at his altar fire:
Come back quickly, for God's love!   1495
Receive from this strange man
Whatever may be his heart's desire
That you and I and Athens are worthy of.
My lord, come quickly as you can!

            (*The thunder continues, until it stops abruptly with
                        the entrance of Theseus, left.*)

SCENE 7

Theseus

Now why do you all together   1500
Set up this shout once more?
I see it comes from you, as from our friend.
Is it a lightning bolt from God? a squall

Of rattling hail? Those are familiar things
When such a tempest rages over heaven.

Oedipus

My lord, I longed for you to come! This is   1505
God's work, your lucky coming.

Theseus

                              Now, what new
Circumstance has arisen, son of Laius?

Oedipus

My life sinks in the scale: I would not die
Without fulfilling what I promised Athens.

Theseus

What proof have you that your hour has come?   1510

Oedipus

The great, incessant thunder and continuous
Flashes of lightning from the hand of God.   1515

Theseus

I believe you. I have seen you prophesy
Many things, none falsely. What must be done?

Oedipus

I shall disclose to you, O son of Aegeus,
What is appointed for you and for your city:
A thing that age will never wear away.
Presently now, without a soul to guide me,   1520
I'll lead you to the place where I must die;
But you must never tell it to any man,
Not even the neighborhood in which it lies.
If you obey, this will count more for you
Than many shields and many neighbors' spears.   1525
These things are mysteries, not to be explained;
But you will understand when you come there
Alone. Alone, because I cannot disclose it
To any of your men or to my children,
Much as I love and cherish them. But you

Keep it secret always, and when you come   1530
To the end of life, then you must hand it on
To your most cherished son, and he in turn
Must teach it to his heir, and so forever.
That way you shall forever hold this city
Safe from the men of Thebes, the dragon's sons.

For every nation that lives peaceably,
There will be many others to grow hard
And push their arrogance to extremes: the gods   1535
Attend to these things slowly. But they attend
To those who put off God and turn to madness!
You have no mind for that, child of Aegeus;
Indeed, you know already all that I teach.

Let us proceed then to that place   1540
And hesitate no longer; I am driven
By an insistent voice that comes from God.
Children, follow me this way: see, now,
I have become your guide, as you were mine!
Come: do not touch me: let me alone discover
The holy and funereal ground where I   1545
Must take this fated earth to be my shroud.

This way, O come! The angel of the dead,
Hermes, and veiled Persephone lead me on!

                    (*He leads them, firmly and slowly, to the left.*)
O sunlight of no light! Once you were mine!
This is the last my flesh will feel of you;   1550
For now I go to shade my ending day
In the dark underworld. Most cherished friend!
I pray that you and this your land and all
Your people may be blessed: remember me,
Be mindful of my death, and be
Fortunate in all the time to come!   1555

            (*Oedipus goes out, followed by his children and by Theseus
                with his Soldiers. The Chorus lifts its arms to pray.*)

CHORAL POEM

Chorus

If I may dare to adore that Lady
The living never see,
And pray to the master of spirits plunged in night,
Who of vast Hell has sovereignty;
Let not our friend go down in grief and weariness   1560
To that all-shrouding cold,
The dead men's plain, the house that has no light.
Because his sufferings were great, unmerited and untold,   1565
Let some just god relieve him from distress!

O powers under the earth, and tameless
Beast in the passage way,   1570
Rumbler prone at the gate of the strange hosts,
Their guard forever, the legends say:
I pray you, even Death, offspring of Earth and Hell,
To let the descent be clear   1575
As Oedipus goes down among the ghosts
On those dim fields of underground that all men living fear.
Eternal sleep, let Oedipus sleep well!

(A long pause. A Messenger comes in, left.)

SCENE 8

Messenger

Citizens, the briefest way to tell you
Would be to say that Oedipus is no more;   1580
But what has happened cannot be told so simply—
It was no simple thing.

Chorus

                    He is gone, poor man?

Messenger

You may be sure that he has left this world.

Chorus

By God's mercy, was his death a painless one?   1585

Messenger

   That is the thing that seems so marvelous.

   You know, for you were witnesses, how he
   Left this place with no friend leading him,
   Acting, himself, as guide for all of us.
   Well, when he came to the steep place in the road,   1590
   The embankment there, secured with steps of brass,
   He stopped in one of the many branching paths.

   This was not far from the stone bowl that marks
   Theseus' and Pirithous' covenant.

   Half-way between that place of stone
   With its hollow pear tree, and the marble tomb,   1595
   He sat down and undid his filthy garments;
   Then he called his daughters and commanded
   That they should bring him water from a fountain
   For bathing and libation to the dead.
   From there they could see the hill of Demeter,   1600
   Freshener of all things: so they ascended it
   And soon came back with water for their father;
   Then helped him properly to bathe and dress.

   When everything was finished to his pleasure,
   And no command of his remained undone,   1605
   Then the earth groaned with thunder from the god below;
   And as they heard the sound, the girls shuddered,
   And dropped to their father's knees, and began wailing,
   Beating their breasts and weeping as if heartbroken.
   And hearing them cry out so bitterly,   1610
   He put his arms around them, and said to them:

  "Children, this day your father is gone from you.
  All that was mine is gone. You shall no longer
  Bear the burden of taking care of me—
  I know it was hard, my children.—And yet one word   1615
  Makes all those difficulties disappear:
  That word is love. You never shall have more

From any man than you have had from me.
And now you must spend the rest of life without me."

That was the way of it. They clung together   1620
And wept, all three. But when they finally stopped,
And no more sobs were heard, then there was
Silence, and in the silence suddenly
A voice cried out to him—of such a kind
It made our hair stand up in panic fear: 1625
Again and again the call came from the god:
"Oedipus! Oedipus! Why are we waiting?
You delay too long; you delay too long to go!"

Then, knowing himself summoned by the spirit,
He asked that the lord Theseus come to him;   1630
And when he had come, said: "O beloved one,
Give your right hand now as a binding pledge
To my two daughters; children, give him your hands.
Promise that you will never willingly
Betray them, but will carry out in kindness
Whatever is best for them in the days to come."   1635

And Theseus swore to do it for his friend,
With such restraint as fits a noble king.
And when he had done so, Oedipus at once
Laid his blind hands upon his daughters, saying:
"Children, you must show your nobility,   1640
And have the courage now to leave this spot.
You must not wish to see what is forbidden,
Or hear what may not afterward be told.
But go—go quickly. Only the lord Theseus
May stay to see the thing that now begins."

This much every one of us heard him say,   1645
And then we came away with the sobbing girls.
But after a little while as we withdrew
We turned around—and nowhere saw that man,
But only the king, his hands before his face,   1650

Shading his eyes as if from something awful,
Fearful and unendurable to see.
Then very quickly we saw him do reverence
To Earth and to the powers of the air,
With one address to both.

But in what manner   1655
Oedipus perished, no one of mortal men
Could tell but Theseus. It was not lightning,
Bearing its fire from God, that took him off;
No hurricane was blowing.   1660
But some attendant from the train of Heaven
Came for him; or else the underworld
Opened in love the unlit door of earth.
For he was taken without lamentation,
Illness or suffering; indeed his end
Was wonderful if mortal's ever was.   1665

Should someone think I speak intemperately,
I make no apology to him who thinks so.

Chorus
But where are his children and the others with them?

Messenger
They are not far away; the sound of weeping
Should tell you now that they are coming here.

(*Antigone and Ismene enter together.*)

CHORAL DIALOGUE

Antigone
Now we may weep, indeed.   1670
Now, if ever, we may cry
In bitter grief against our fate,
Our heritage still unappeased.
In other days we stood up under it,
Endured it for his sake,
The unrelenting horror. Now the finish   1675
Comes, and we know only

In all that we have seen and done
Bewildering mystery.

Chorus

What happened?

Antigone

We can only guess, my friends.

Chorus

He has gone?

Antigone

He has; as one could wish him to.
Why not? It was not war
Nor the deep sea that overtook him,   1680
But something invisible and strange
Caught him up—or down—
Into a space unseen.
But we are lost. A deathly
Night is ahead of us.
For how, in some far country wandering,   1685
Or on the lifting seas,
Shall we eke out our lives?

Ismene

I cannot guess. But as for me
I wish that charnel Hell would take me   1690
In one death with our father.
This is such desolation
I cannot go on living.

Chorus

Most admirable sisters:
Whatever God has brought about
Is to be borne with courage.
You must not feed the flames of grief.   1695
No blame can come to you.

Antigone

One may long for the past
Though at the time indeed it seemed

Nothing but wretchedness and evil.
Life was not sweet, yet I found it so
When I could put my arms around my father.
O father! O my dear!
Now you are shrouded in eternal darkness,
Even in that absence
You shall not lack our love,
Mine and my sister's love.

Chorus

He lived his life.

Antigone

He did as he had wished!

Chorus

What do you mean?

Antigone

In this land among strangers
He died where he chose to die.
He has his eternal bed well shaded,
And in his death is not unmourned.
My eyes are blind with tears
From crying for you, father.
The terror and the loss
Cannot be quieted.
I know you wished to die in a strange country,
Yet your death was so lonely!
Why could I not be with you?

Ismene

O pity! What is left for me?
What destiny awaits us both
Now we have lost our father?

Chorus

Dear children, remember
That his last hour was free and blessed.
So make an end of grieving!

1700

1705

1710

1715

1720

Is anyone in all the world
Safe from unhappiness?

Antigone
Let us run back there!

Ismene
Why, what shall we do?

Antigone
I am carried away with longing—

Ismene
For what,—tell me!   1725

Antigone
To see the resting place in the earth—

Ismene
Of whom?

Antigone
Oh, father's! O dear God, I am so unhappy!

Ismene
But that is not permitted. Do you not see?

Antigone
Do not rebuke me!

Ismene
—And remember, too—   1730

Antigone
Oh, what?

Ismene
He had no tomb, there was no one near!

Antigone
Take me there and you can kill me, too!

Ismene
Ah! I am truly lost!
Helpless and so forsaken!   1735
Where shall I go and how shall I live?

Chorus
Don't be afraid, now.

Antigone

                    Yes, but where is a refuge?

Chorus

  A refuge has been found—

Antigone

                   Where do you mean?

Chorus

  A place where you will be unharmed!

Antigone

                   No ...   1740

Chorus

  What are you thinking?

Antigone

                I think there is no way
  For me to get home again.

Chorus

              Do not go home!

Antigone

  My home is in trouble.

Chorus

            So it has been before.

Antigone

  There was no help for it then: but now it is worse.   1745

Chorus

  A wide and desolate world it is for you.

Antigone

  Great God! What way is there?
  Do the powers that rule our lives
  Still press me on to hope at all?   1750

              (Theseus comes in, with attendants.)

Theseus

  Mourn no more, children. Those to whom
  The night of earth gives benediction
  Should not be mourned. Retribution comes.

Antigone

  Theseus: we fall on our knees to you!

Theseus
  What is it that you desire, children?   1755

Antigone
  We wish to see the place ourselves
  In which our father rests.

Theseus
              No, no.
  It is not permissible to go there.

Antigone
  My lord and ruler of Athens, why?

Theseus
  Because your father told me, children,   1760
  That no one should go near the spot,
  No mortal man should tell of it,
  Since it is holy, and is his.
  And if I kept this pledge, he said,
  I should preserve my land from its enemies.   1765
  I swore I would, and the god heard me:
  The oathkeeper who keeps track of all.

Antigone
  If this was our father's cherished wish,
  We must be satisfied.
  Send us back, then, to ancient Thebes,   1770
  And we may stop the bloody war
  From coming between our brothers!

Theseus
  I will do that, and whatever else
  I am able to do for your happiness,
  For his sake who has gone just now   1775
  Beneath the earth. I must not fail.

Chorus
  Now let the weeping cease;
  Let no one mourn again.
  These things are in the hands of God.

ANTIGONE

Translated by Elizabeth Wyckoff

CHARACTERS

Antigone

Ismene

Chorus of Theban Elders

Creon

A Guard

Haemon

Teiresias

A Messenger

Eurydice

ANTIGONE

Scene: *Thebes, before the royal palace. Antigone and Ismene emerge from its great central door.*

Antigone

My sister, my Ismene, do you know
of any suffering from our father sprung
that Zeus does not achieve for us survivors?
There's nothing grievous, nothing free from doom,
not shameful, not dishonored, I've not seen.
Your sufferings and mine.
And now, what of this edict which they say
the commander has proclaimed to the whole people?
Have you heard anything? Or don't you know
that the foes' trouble comes upon our friends?   10

Ismene

I've heard no word, Antigone, of our friends.
Not sweet nor bitter, since that single moment
when we two lost two brothers
who died on one day by a double blow.
And since the Argive army went away
this very night, I have no further news
of fortune or disaster for myself.

Antigone

I knew it well, and brought you from the house
for just this reason, that you alone may hear.

Ismene

What is it? Clearly some news has clouded you.   20

Antigone

It has indeed. Creon will give the one
of our two brothers honor in the tomb;
the other none.

Eteocles, with just entreatment treated,
as law provides he has hidden under earth
to have full honor with the dead below.
But Polyneices' corpse who died in pain,
they say he has proclaimed to the whole town
that none may bury him and none bewail,
but leave him unwept, untombed, a rich sweet sight
for the hungry birds' beholding.   30
Such orders they say the worthy Creon gives
to you and me—yes, yes, I say to *me*—
and that he's coming to proclaim it clear
to those who know it not.
Further: he has the matter so at heart
that anyone who dares attempt the act
will die by public stoning in the town.
So there you have it and you soon will show
if you are noble, or fallen from your descent.

Ismene
If things have reached this stage, what can I do,
poor sister, that will help to make or mend?   40

Antigone
Think will you share my labor and my act.

Ismene
What will you risk? And where is your intent?

Antigone
Will you take up that corpse along with me?

Ismene
To bury him you mean, when it's forbidden?

Antigone
My brother, and yours, though you may wish he were not.
I never shall be found to be his traitor.

Ismene
O hard of mind! When Creon spoke against it!

Antigone

    It's not for him to keep me from my own.

Ismene

    Alas. Remember, sister, how our father
    perished abhorred, ill-famed.   50
    Himself with his own hand, through his own curse
    destroyed both eyes.
    Remember next his mother and his wife
    finishing life in the shame of the twisted strings.
    And third two brothers on a single day,
    poor creatures, murdering, a common doom
    each with his arm accomplished on the other.
    And now look at the two of us alone.
    We'll perish terribly if we force law
    and try to cross the royal vote and power.   60
    We must remember that we two are women
    so not to fight with men.
    And that since we are subject to strong power
    we must hear these orders, or any that may be worse.
    So I shall ask of them beneath the earth
    forgiveness, for in these things I am forced,
    and shall obey the men in power. I know
    that wild and futile action makes no sense.

Antigone

    I wouldn't urge it. And if now you wished
    to act, you wouldn't please me as a partner.   70
    Be what you want to; but that man shall I
    bury. For me, the doer, death is best.
    Friend shall I lie with him, yes friend with friend,
    when I have dared the crime of piety.
    Longer the time in which to please the dead
    than that for those up here.
    There shall I lie forever. You may see fit
    to keep from honor what the gods have honored.

Ismene

> I shall do no dishonor. But to act
> against the citizens. I cannot.

Antigone

> That's your protection. Now I go, to pile   80
> the burial-mound for him, my dearest brother.

Ismene

> Oh my poor sister. How I fear for you!

Antigone

> For me, don't borrow trouble. Clear your fate.

Ismene

> At least give no one warning of this act;
> you keep it hidden, and I'll do the same.

Antigone

> Dear God! Denounce me. I shall hate you more
> if silent, not proclaiming this to all.

Ismene

> You have a hot mind over chilly things.

Antigone

> I know I please those whom I most should please.

Ismene

> If but you can. You crave what can't be done.   90

Antigone

> And so, when strength runs out, I shall give over.

Ismene

> Wrong from the start, to chase what cannot be.

Antigone

> If that's your saying, I shall hate you first,
> and next the dead will hate you in all justice.
> But let me and my own ill-counselling
> suffer this terror. I shall suffer nothing
> as great as dying with a lack of grace.

Ismene

Go, since you want to. But know this: you go
senseless indeed, but loved by those who love you.

(*Ismene returns to the palace; Antigone leaves by one of the side
entrances. The Chorus now enters from the other side.*)

Chorus

Sun's own radiance, fairest light ever shone on the gates of
Thebes,   100
then did you shine, O golden day's
eye, coming over Dirce's stream,
on the Man who had come from Argos with all his armor
running now in headlong fear as you shook his bridle free.

He was stirred by the dubious quarrel of Polyneices.   110
So, screaming shrill,
like an eagle over the land he flew,
covered with white-snow wing,
with many weapons,
with horse-hair crested helms.

He who had stood above our halls, gaping about our seven gates,
with that circle of thirsting spears.
Gone, without our blood in his jaws,   120
before the torch took hold on our tower-crown.
Rattle of war at his back; hard the fight for the dragon's foe.

The boasts of a proud tongue are for Zeus to hate.
So seeing them streaming on
in insolent clangor of gold,   130
he struck with hurling fire him who rushed
for the high wall's top,
to cry conquest abroad.

Swinging, striking the earth he fell
fire in hand, who in mad attack,
had raged against us with blasts of hate.
He failed. He failed of his aim.

For the rest great Ares dealt his blows about,
first in the war-team.   140

    The captains stationed at seven gates
    fought with seven and left behind
    their brazen arms as an offering
    to Zeus who is turner of battle.
    All but those wretches, sons of one man,
    one mother's sons, who sent their spears
    each against each and found the share
    of a common death together.

Great-named Victory comes to us
answering Thebe's warrior-joy.
Let us forget the wars just done   150
and visit the shrines of the gods.
All, with night-long dance which Bacchus will lead,
who shakes Thebe's acres.

                              (Creon enters from the palace.)

    Now here he comes, the king of the land,
    Creon, Menoeceus' son,
    newly named by the gods' new fate.
    What plan that beats about his mind
    has made him call this council-session,   160
    sending his summons to all?

Creon
    My friends, the very gods who shook the state
    with mighty surge have set it straight again.
    So nòw I sent for you, chosen from all,
    first that I knew you constant in respect
    to Laius' royal power; and again
    when Oedipus had set the state to rights,
    and when he perished, you were faithful still
    in mind to the descendants of the dead.
    When they two perished by a double fate,   170
    on one day struck and striking and defiled
    each by his own hand, now it comes that I

hold all the power and the royal throne
through close connection with the perished men.
You cannot learn of any man the soul,
the mind, and the intent until he shows
his practise of the government and law.
For I believe that who controls the state
and does not hold to the best plans of all,
but locks his tongue up through some kind of fear,   180
that he is worst of all who are or were.
And he who counts another greater friend
than his own fatherland, I put him nowhere.
So I—may Zeus all-seeing always know it—
could not keep silent as disaster crept
upon the town, destroying hope of safety.
Nor could I count the enemy of the land
friend to myself, not I who know so well
that she it is who saves us, sailing straight,
and only so can we have friends at all.   190
With such good rules shall I enlarge our state.
And now I have proclaimed their brother-edict.
In the matter of the sons of Oedipus,
citizens, know: Eteocles who died,
defending this our town with champion spear,
is to be covered in the grave and granted
all holy rites we give the noble dead.
But his brother Polyneices whom I name
the exile who came back and sought to burn   200
his fatherland, the gods who were his kin,
who tried to gorge on blood he shared, and lead
the rest of us as slaves—
it is announced that no one in this town
may give him burial or mourn for him.
Leave him unburied, leave his corpse disgraced,
a dinner for the birds and for the dogs.
Such is my mind. Never shall I, myself,
honor the wicked and reject the just.

The man who is well-minded to the state
from me in death and life shall have his honor.   210

Chorus

This resolution, Creon, is your own,
in the matter of the traitor and the true.
For you can make such rulings as you will
about the living and about the dead.

Creon

Now you be sentinels of the decree.

Chorus

Order some younger man to take this on.

Creon

Already there are watchers of the corpse.

Chorus

What other order would you give us, then?

Creon

Not to take sides with any who disobey.

Chorus

No fool is fool as far as loving death.   220

Creon

Death is the price. But often we have known
men to be ruined by the hope of profit.

(Enter, from the side, a guard.)

Guard

Lord, I can't claim that I am out of breath
from rushing here with light and hasty step,
for I had many haltings in my thought
making me double back upon my road.
My mind kept saying many things to me:
"Why go where you will surely pay the price?"
"Fool, are you halting? And if Creon learns
from someone else, how shall you not be hurt?"   230
Turning this over, on I dilly-dallied.

And so a short trip turns itself to long.
Finally, though, my coming here won out.
If what I say is nothing, still I'll say it.
For I come clutching to one single hope
that I can't suffer what is not my fate.

Creon

What is it that brings on this gloom of yours?

Guard

I want to tell you first about myself.
I didn't do it, didn't see who did it.
It isn't right for me to get in trouble.   240

Creon

Your aim is good. You fence the fact around.
It's clear you have some shocking news to tell.

Guard

Terrible tidings make for long delays.

Creon

Speak out the story, and then get away.

Guard

I'll tell you. Someone left the corpse just now,
burial all accomplished, thirsty dust
strewn on the flesh, the ritual complete.

Creon

What are you saying? What man has dared to do it?

Guard

I wouldn't know. There were no marks of picks,
no grubbed-out earth. The ground was dry and hard,   250
no trace of wheels. The doer left no sign.
When the first fellow on the day-shift showed us,
we all were sick with wonder.
For he was hidden, not inside a tomb,
light dust upon him, enough to turn the curse,
no wild beast's track, nor track of any hound

having been near, nor was the body torn.
We roared bad words about, guard against guard, 260
and came to blows. No one was there to stop us.
Each man had done it, nobody had done it
so as to prove it on him—we couldn't tell.
We were prepared to hold to red-hot iron,
to walk through fire, to swear before the gods
we hadn't done it, hadn't shared the plan,
when it was plotted or when it was done.
And last, when all our sleuthing came out nowhere,
one fellow spoke, who made our heads to droop
low toward the ground. We couldn't disagree. 270
We couldn't see a chance of getting off.
He said we had to tell you all about it.
We couldn't hide the fact.
So he won out. The lot chose poor old me
to win the prize. So here I am unwilling,
quite sure you people hardly want to see me.
Nobody likes the bringer of bad news.

Chorus

Lord, while he spoke, my mind kept on debating.
Isn't this action possibly a god's?

Creon

Stop now, before you fill me up with rage, 280
or you'll prove yourself insane as well as old.
Unbearable, your saying that the gods
take any kindly forethought for this corpse.
Would it be they had hidden him away,
honoring his good service, his who came
to burn their pillared temples and their wealth,
even their land, and break apart their laws?
Or have you seen them honor wicked men?
It isn't so.
No, from the first there were some men in town 290
who took the edict hard, and growled against me,

who hid the fact that they were rearing back,
not rightly in the yoke, no way my friends.
These are the people—oh it's clear to me—
who have bribed these men and brought about the deed.
No current custom among men as bad
as silver currency. This destroys the state;
this drives men from their homes; this wicked teacher
drives solid citizens to acts of shame.
It shows men how to practise infamy   300
and know the deeds of all unholiness.
Every least hireling who helped in this
brought about then the sentence he shall have.
But further, as I still revere great Zeus,
understand this, I tell you under oath,
if you don't find the very man whose hands
buried the corpse, bring him for me to see,
not death alone shall be enough for you
till living, hanging, you make clear the crime.
For any future grabbings you'll have learned   310
where to get pay, and that it doesn't pay
to squeeze a profit out of every source.
For you'll have felt that more men come to doom
through dirty profits than are kept by them.

Guard
    May I say something? Or just turn and go?

Creon
    Aren't you aware your speech is most unwelcome?

Guard
    Does it annoy your hearing or your mind?

Creon
    Why are you out to allocate my pain?

Guard
    The doer hurts your mind. I hurt your ears.

Creon

You are a quibbling rascal through and through.   320

Guard

But anyhow I never did the deed.

Creon

And you the man who sold your mind for money!

Guard

Oh!
How terrible to guess, and guess at lies!

Creon

Go pretty up your guesswork. If you don't
show me the doers you will have to say
that wicked payments work their own revenge.

Guard

Indeed, I pray he's found, but yes or no,
taken or not as luck may settle it,
you won't see me returning to this place.
Saved when I neither hoped nor thought to be,   330
I owe the gods a mighty debt of thanks.

(*Creon enters the palace. The Guard leaves by the way he came.*)

Chorus

Many the wonders but nothing walks stranger than man.
This thing crosses the sea in the winter's storm,
making his path through the roaring waves.
And she, the greatest of gods, the earth—
ageless she is, and unwearied—he wears her away
as the ploughs go up and down from year to year   340
and his mules turn up the soil.

Gay nations of birds he snares and leads,
wild beast tribes and the salty brood of the sea,
with the twisted mesh of his nets, this clever man.
He controls with craft the beasts of the open air,
walkers on hills. The horse with his shaggy mane   350

he holds and harnesses, yoked about the neck,
and the strong bull of the mountain.

Language, and thought like the wind
and the feelings that make the town,
he has taught himself, and shelter against the cold,
refuge from rain. He can always help himself.
He faces no future helpless. There's only death
that he cannot find an escape from. He has contrived   360
refuge from illnesses once beyond all cure.

Clever beyond all dreams
the inventive craft that he has
which may drive him one time or another to well or ill.
When he honors the laws of the land and the gods' sworn right
high indeed is his city; but stateless the man   370
who dares to dwell with dishonor. Not by my fire,
never to share my thoughts, who does these things.

(The Guard enters with Antigone.)

My mind is split at this awful sight.
I know her. I cannot deny
Antigone is here.
Alas, the unhappy girl,
her unhappy father's child.
Oh what is the meaning of this?   380
It cannot be you that they bring
for breaking the royal law,
caught in open shame.

Guard

This is the woman who has done the deed.
We caught her at the burying. Where's the king?

(Creon enters.)

Chorus

Back from the house again just when he's needed.

Creon

What must I measure up to? What has happened?

Guard

    Lord, one should never swear off anything.
    Afterthought makes the first resolve a liar.
    I could have vowed I wouldn't come back here   390
    after your threats, after the storm I faced.
    But joy that comes beyond the wildest hope
    is bigger than all other pleasure known.
    I'm here, though I swore not to be, and bring
    this girl. We caught her burying the dead.
    This time we didn't need to shake the lots;
    mine was the luck, all mine.
    So now, lord, take her, you, and question her
    and prove her as you will. But I am free.
    And I deserve full clearance on this charge.   400

Creon

    Explain the circumstance of the arrest.

Guard

    She was burying the man. You have it all.

Creon

    Is this the truth? And do you grasp its meaning?

Guard

    I saw her burying the very corpse
    you had forbidden. Is this adequate?

Creon

    How was she caught and taken in the act?

Guard

    It was like this: when we got back again
    struck with those dreadful threatenings of yours,
    we swept away the dust that hid the corpse.   410
    We stripped it back to slimy nakedness.
    And then we sat to windward on the hill
    so as to dodge the smell.
    We poked each other up with growling threats
    if anyone was careless of his work.

For some time this went on, till it was noon.
The sun was high and hot. Then from the earth
up rose a dusty whirlwind to the sky,
filling the plain, smearing the forest-leaves,
clogging the upper air. We shut our eyes,   420
sat and endured the plague the gods had sent.
So the storm left us after a long time.
We saw the girl. She cried the sharp and shrill
cry of a bitter bird which sees the nest
bare where the young birds lay.
So this same girl, seeing the body stripped,
cried with great groanings, cried a dreadful curse
upon the people who had done the deed.
Soon in her hands she brought the thirsty dust,
and holding high a pitcher of wrought bronze   430
she poured the three libations for the dead.
We saw this and surged down. We trapped her fast;
and she was calm. We taxed her with the deeds
both past and present. Nothing was denied.
And I was glad, and yet I took it hard.
One's own escape from trouble makes one glad;
but bringing friends to trouble is hard grief.
Still, I care less for all these second thoughts
than for the fact that I myself am safe.   440

Creon
    You there, whose head is drooping to the ground,
    do you admit this, or deny you did it?

Antigone
    I say I did it and I don't deny it.

Creon (to the guard)
    Take yourself off wherever you wish to go
    free of a heavy charge.

Creon (to Antigone)
    You—tell me not at length but in a word.
    You knew the order not to do this thing?

Antigone

  I knew, of course I knew. The word was plain.

Creon

  And still you dared to overstep these laws?

Antigone

  For me it was not Zeus who made that order.   450
  Nor did that Justice who lives with the gods below
  mark out such laws to hold among mankind.
  Nor did I think your orders were so strong
  that you, a mortal man, could over-run
  the gods' unwritten and unfailing laws.
  Not now, nor yesterday's, they always live,
  and no one knows their origin in time.
  So not through fear of any man's proud spirit
  would I be likely to neglect these laws,
  draw on myself the gods' sure punishment.
  I knew that I must die; how could I not?   460
  even without your warning. If I die
  before my time, I say it is a gain.
  Who lives in sorrows many as are mine
  how shall he not be glad to gain his death?
  And so, for me to meet this fate, no grief.
  But if I left that corpse, my mother's son,
  dead and unburied I'd have cause to grieve
  as now I grieve not.
  And if you think my acts are foolishness
  the foolishness may be in a fool's eye.   470

Chorus

  The girl is bitter. She's her father's child.
  She cannot yield to trouble; nor could he.

Creon

  These rigid spirits are the first to fall.
  The strongest iron, hardened in the fire,
  most often ends in scraps and shatterings.

Small curbs bring raging horses back to terms.
Slave to his neighbor, who can think of pride?
This girl was expert in her insolence   480
when she broke bounds beyond established law.
Once she had done it, insolence the second,
to boast her doing, and to laugh in it.
I am no man and she the man instead
if she can have this conquest without pain.
She is my sister's child, but were she child
of closer kin than any at my hearth,
she and her sister should not so escape
their death and doom. I charge Ismene too.
She shared the planning of this burial.   490
Call her outside. I saw her in the house,
maddened, no longer mistress of herself.
The sly intent betrays itself sometimes
before the secret plotters work their wrong.
I hate it too when someone caught in crime
then wants to make it seem a lovely thing.

Antigone

Do you want more than my arrest and death?

Creon

No more than that. For that is all I need.

Antigone

Why are you waiting? Nothing that you say
fits with my thought. I pray it never will.   500
Nor will you ever like to hear my words.
And yet what greater glory could I find
than giving my own brother funeral?
All these would say that they approved my act
did fear not mute them.
(A king is fortunate in many ways,
and most, that he can act and speak at will.)

Creon

None of these others see the case this way.

Antigone

They see, and do not say. You have them cowed.

Creon

And you are not ashamed to think alone? 510

Antigone

No, I am not ashamed. When was it shame
to serve the children of my mother's womb?

Creon

It was not your brother who died against him, then?

Antigone

Full brother, on both sides, my parents' child.

Creon

Your act of grace, in his regard, is crime.

Antigone

The corpse below would never say it was.

Creon

When you honor him and the criminal just alike?

Antigone

It was a brother, not a slave, who died.

Creon

Died to destroy this land the other guarded.

Antigone

Death yearns for equal law for all the dead.

Creon

Not that the good and bad draw equal shares. 520

Antigone

Who knows that this is holiness below?

Creon

Never the enemy, even in death, a friend.

Antigone

I cannot share in hatred, but in love.

Creon

    Then go down there, if you must love, and love
    the dead. No woman rules me while I live.

               (Ismene is brought from the palace under guard.)

Chorus

    Look there! Ismene is coming out.
    She loves her sister and mourns,
    with clouded brow and bloodied cheeks,
    tears on her lovely face. 530

Creon

    You, lurking like a viper in the house,
    who sucked me dry. I looked the other way
    while twin destruction planned against the throne.
    Now tell me, do you say you shared this deed?
    Or will you swear you didn't even know?

Ismene

    I did the deed, if she agrees I did.
    I am accessory and share the blame.

Antigone

    Justice will not allow this. You did not
    wish for a part, nor did I give you one.

Ismene

    You are in trouble, and I'm not ashamed 540
    to sail beside you into suffering.

Antigone

    Death and the dead, they know whose act it was.
    I cannot love a friend whose love is words.

Ismene

    Sister, I pray, don't fence me out from honor,
    from death with you, and honor done the dead.

Antigone

    Don't die along with me, nor make your own
    that which you did not do. My death's enough.

Ismene

When you are gone what life can be my friend?

Antigone

Love Creon. He's your kinsman and your care.

Ismene

Why hurt me, when it does yourself no good? 550

Antigone

I also suffer, when I laugh at you.

Ismene

What further service can I do you now?

Antigone

To save yourself. I shall not envy you.

Ismene

Alas for me. Am I outside your fate?

Antigone

Yes. For you chose to live when I chose death.

Ismene

At least I was not silent. You were warned.

Antigone

Some will have thought you wiser. Some will not.

Ismene

And yet the blame is equal for us both.

Antigone

Take heart. You live. My life died long ago.
And that has made me fit to help the dead. 560

Creon

One of these girls has shown her lack of sense
just now. The other had it from her birth.

Ismene

Yes, lord. When people fall in deep distress
their native sense departs, and will not stay.

Creon
> You chose your mind's distraction when you chose
> to work out wickedness with this wicked girl.

Ismene
> What life is there for me to live without her?

Creon
> Don't speak of her. For she is here no more.

Ismene
> But will you kill your own son's promised bride?

Creon
> Oh, there are other furrows for his plough.

Ismene
> But where the closeness that has bound these two?   570

Creon
> Not for my sons will I choose wicked wives.

Ismene
> Dear Haemon, your father robs you of your rights.

Creon
> You and your marriage trouble me too much.

Ismene
> You will take away his bride from your own son?

Creon
> Yes. Death will help me break this marriage off.

Chorus
> It seems determined that the girl must die.

Creon
> You helped determine it. Now, no delay!
> Slaves, take them in. They must be women now.
> No more free running.
> Even the bold will fly when they see Death   580
> drawing in close enough to end their life.

(Antigone and Ismene are taken inside.)

Chorus

Fortunate they whose lives have no taste of pain.
For those whose house is shaken by the gods
escape no kind of doom. It extends to all the kin
like the wave that comes when the winds of Thrace
run over the dark of the sea.
The black sand of the bottom is brought from the depth;   590
the beaten capes sound back with a hollow cry.

Ancient the sorrow of Labdacus' house, I know.
Dead men's grief comes back, and falls on grief.
No generation can free the next.
One of the gods will strike. There is no escape.
So now the light goes out
for the house of Oedipus, while the bloody knife   600
cuts the remaining root. Folly and Fury have done this.

What madness of man, O Zeus, can bind your power?
Not sleep can destroy it who ages all,
nor the weariless months the gods have set. Unaged in time
monarch you rule of Olympus' gleaming light.   610
Near time, far future, and the past,
one law controls them all:
any greatness in human life brings doom.

Wandering hope brings help to many men.
But others she tricks from their giddy loves,
and her quarry knows nothing until he has walked into flame.
Word of wisdom it was when someone said,   620
"The bad becomes the good
to him a god would doom."
Only briefly is that one from under doom.

(Haemon enters from the side.)

Here is your one surviving son.
Does he come in grief at the fate of his bride,
in pain that he's tricked of his wedding?   630

Creon

  Soon we shall know more than a seer could tell us.
  Son, have you heard the vote condemned your bride?
  And are you here, maddened against your father,
  or are we friends, whatever I may do?

Haemon

  My father, I am yours. You keep me straight
  with your good judgment, which I shall ever follow.
  Nor shall a marriage count for more with me
  than your kind leading.

Creon

  There's my good boy. So should you hold at heart
  and stand behind your father all the way.   640
  It is for this men pray they may beget
  households of dutiful obedient sons,
  who share alike in punishing enemies,
  and give due honor to their father's friends.
  Whoever breeds a child that will not help
  what has he sown but trouble for himself,
  and for his enemies laughter full and free?
  Son, do not let your lust mislead your mind,
  all for a woman's sake, for well you know
  how cold the thing he takes into his arms   650
  who has a wicked woman for his wife.
  What deeper wounding than a friend no friend?
  Oh spit her forth forever, as your foe.
  Let the girl marry somebody in Hades.
  Since I have caught her in the open act,
  the only one in town who disobeyed,
  I shall not now proclaim myself a liar,
  but kill her. Let her sing her song of Zeus
  who guards the kindred.
  If I allow disorder in my house
  I'd surely have to licence it abroad.   660
  A man who deals in fairness with his own,

he can make manifest justice in the state.
But he who crosses law, or forces it,
or hopes to bring the rulers under him,
shall never have a word of praise from me.
The man the state has put in place must have
obedient hearing to his least command
when it is right, and even when it's not.
He who accepts this teaching I can trust,
ruler, or ruled, to function in his place,
to stand his ground even in the storm of spears,   670
a mate to trust in battle at one's side.
There is no greater wrong than disobedience.
This ruins cities, this tears down our homes,
this breaks the battle-front in panic-rout.
If men live decently it is because
discipline saves their very lives for them.
So I must guard the men who yield to order,
not let myself be beaten by a woman.
Better, if it must happen, that a man
should overset me.
I won't be called weaker than womankind.   680

Chorus
      We think—unless our age is cheating us—
      that what you say is sensible and right.

Haemon
      Father, the gods have given men good sense,
      the only sure possession that we have.
      I couldn't find the words in which to claim
      that there was error in your late remarks.
      Yet someone else might bring some further light.
      Because I am your son I must keep watch
      on all men's doing where it touches you,
      their speech, and most of all, their discontents.
      Your presence frightens any common man   690
      from saying things you would not care to hear.

But in dark corners I have heard them say
how the whole town is grieving for this girl,
unjustly doomed, if ever woman was,
to die in shame for glorious action done.
She would not leave her fallen, slaughtered brother
there, as he lay, unburied, for the birds
and hungry dogs to make an end of him.
Isn't her real desert a golden prize?
This is the undercover speech in town.   700
Father, your welfare is my greatest good.
What loveliness in life for any child
outweighs a father's fortune and good fame?
And so a father feels his children's faring.
Then, do not have one mind, and one alone
that only your opinion can be right.
Whoever thinks that he alone is wise,
his eloquence, his mind, above the rest,
come the unfolding, shows his emptiness.
A man, though wise, should never be ashamed   710
of learning more, and must unbend his mind.
Have you not seen the trees beside the torrent,
the ones that bend them saving every leaf,
while the resistant perish root and branch?
And so the ship that will not slacken sail,
the sheet drawn tight, unyielding, overturns.
She ends the voyage with her keel on top.
No, yield your wrath, allow a change of stand.
Young as I am, if I may give advice,
I'd say it would be best if men were born   720
perfect in wisdom, but that failing this
(which often fails) it can be no dishonor
to learn from others when they speak good sense.

Chorus

Lord, if your son has spoken to the point
you should take his lesson. He should do the same.
Both sides have spoken well.

Creon

    At my age I'm to school my mind by his?
    This boy instructor is my master, then?

Haemon

    I urge no wrong. I'm young, but you should watch
    my actions, not my years, to judge of me.

Creon

    A loyal action, to respect disorder?   730

Haemon

    I wouldn't urge respect for wickedness.

Creon

    You don't think she is sick with that disease?

Haemon

    Your fellow-citizens maintain she's not.

Creon

    Is the town to tell me how I ought to rule?

Haemon

    Now there you speak just like a boy yourself.

Creon

    Am I to rule by other mind than mine?

Haemon

    No city is property of a single man.

Creon

    But custom gives possession to the ruler.

Haemon

    You'd rule a desert beautifully alone.

Creon (*to the Chorus*)

    It seems he's firmly on the woman's side.   740

Haemon

    If you're a woman. It is you I care for.

Creon

    Wicked, to try conclusions with your father.

Haemon
    When you conclude unjustly, so I must.

Creon
    Am I unjust, when I respect my office?

Haemon
    You tread down the gods' due. Respect is gone.

Creon
    Your mind is poisoned. Weaker than a woman!

Haemon
    At least you'll never see me yield to shame.

Creon
    Your whole long argument is but for her.

Haemon
    And you, and me, and for the gods below.

Creon
    You shall not marry her while she's alive.   750

Haemon
    Then she shall die. Her death will bring another.

Creon
    Your boldness has made progress. Threats, indeed!

Haemon
    No threat, to speak against your empty plan.

Creon
    Past due, sharp lessons for your empty brain.

Haemon
    If you weren't father, I should call you mad.

Creon
    Don't flatter me with "father," you woman's slave.

Haemon
    You wish to speak but never wish to hear.

Creon
    You think so? By Olympus, you shall not
    revile me with these tauntings and go free.

Bring out the hateful creature; she shall die
full in his sight, close at her bridegroom's side.   760

Haemon

Not at my side her death, and you will not
ever lay eyes upon my face again.
Find other friends to rave with after this.

                    (*Haemon leaves, by one of the side entrances.*)

Chorus

Lord, he has gone with all the speed of rage.
When such a man is grieved his mind is hard.

Creon

Oh, let him go, plan superhuman action.
In any case the girls shall not escape.

Chorus

You plan for both the punishment of death?   770

Creon

Not her who did not do it. You are right.

Chorus

And what death have you chosen for the other?

Creon

To take her where the foot of man comes not.
There shall I hide her in a hollowed cave
living, and leave her just so much to eat
as clears the city from the guilt of death.
There, if she prays to Death, the only god
of her respect, she may manage not to die.
Or she may learn at last and even then
how much too much her labor for the dead.   780

                    (*Creon returns to the palace.*)

Chorus

Love unconquered in fight, love who falls on our havings.
You rest in the bloom of a girl's unwithered face.
You cross the sea, you are known in the wildest lairs.

Not the immortal gods can fly,
nor men of a day. Who has you within him is mad.   790

You twist the minds of the just. Wrong they pursue and are
    ruined.
You made this quarrel of kindred before us now.
Desire looks clear from the eyes of a lovely bride:
power as strong as the founded world.
For there is the goddess at play with whom no man can fight.   800

    (Antigone is brought from the palace under guard.)

Now I am carried beyond all bounds.
My tears will not be checked.
I see Antigone depart
to the chamber where all men sleep.

Antigone

Men of my fathers' land, you see me go
my last journey. My last sight of the sun,
then never again. Death who brings all to sleep   810
takes me alive to the shore
of the river underground.
Not for me was the marriage-hymn, nor will anyone start the
    song
at a wedding of mine. Acheron is my mate.

Chorus

With praise as your portion you go
in fame to the vault of the dead.
Untouched by wasting disease,
not paying the price of the sword,   820
of your own motion you go.
Alone among mortals will you descend
in life to the house of Death.

Antigone

Pitiful was the death that stranger died,
our queen once, Tantalus' daughter. The rock
it covered her over, like stubborn ivy it grew.

Still, as she wastes, the rain
and snow companion her.
Pouring down from her mourning eyes comes the water that
    soaks the stone.   830
My own putting to sleep a god has planned like hers.

Chorus

    God's child and god she was.
    We are born to death.
    Yet even in death you will have your fame,
    to have gone like a god to your fate,
    in living and dying alike.

Antigone

    Laughter against me now. In the name of our fathers' gods,
    could you not wait till I went? Must affront be thrown in my
        face?   840
    O city of wealthy men.
    I call upon Dirce's spring,
    I call upon Thebe's grove in the armored plain,
    to be my witnesses, how with no friend's mourning,
    by what decree I go to the fresh-made prison-tomb.
    Alive to the place of corpses, an alien still,   850
    never at home with the living nor with the dead.

Chorus

    You went to the furthest verge
    of daring, but there you found
    the high foundation of justice, and fell.
    Perhaps you are paying your father's pain.

Antigone

    You speak of my darkest thought, my pitiful father's fame,
    spread through all the world, and the doom that haunts our
        house,   860
    the royal house of Thebes.
    My mother's marriage-bed.
    Destruction where she lay with her husband-son,
    my father. These are my parents and I their child.

I go to stay with them. My curse is to die unwed.
My brother, you found your fate when you found your bride,   870
found it for me as well. Dead, you destroy my life.

Chorus

You showed respect for the dead.
So we for you: but power
is not to be thwarted so.
Your self-sufficiency has brought you down.

Antigone

Unwept, no wedding-song, unfriended, now I go
the road laid down for me.
No longer shall I see this holy light of the sun.   880
No friend to bewail my fate.

(*Creon enters from the palace.*)

Creon

When people sing the dirge for their own deaths
ahead of time, nothing will break them off
if they can hope that this will buy delay.
Take her away at once, and open up
the tomb I spoke of. Leave her there alone.
There let her choose: death, or a buried life.
No stain of guilt upon us in this case,
but she is exiled from our life on earth.   890

Antigone

O tomb, O marriage-chamber, hollowed out
house that will watch forever, where I go.
To my own people, who are mostly there;
Persephone has taken them to her.
Last of them all, ill-fated past the rest,
shall I descend, before my course is run.
Still when I get there I may hope to find
I come as a dear friend to my dear father,
to you, my mother, and my brother too.
All three of you have known my hand in death.   900
I washed your bodies, dressed them for the grave,

poured out the last libation at the tomb.
Last, Polyneices knows the price I pay
for doing final service to his corpse.
And yet the wise will know my choice was right.
Had I had children or their father dead,
I'd let them moulder. I should not have chosen
in such a case to cross the state's decree.
What is the law that lies behind these words?
One husband gone, I might have found another,
or a child from a new man in first child's place,   910
but with my parents hid away in death,
no brother, ever, could spring up for me.
Such was the law by which I honored you.
But Creon thought the doing was a crime,
a dreadful daring, brother of my heart.
So now he takes and leads me out by force.
No marriage-bed, no marriage-song for me,
and since no wedding, so no child to rear.
I go, without a friend, struck down by fate,
live to the hollow chambers of the dead.   920
What divine justice have I disobeyed?
Why, in my misery, look to the gods for help?
Can I call any of them my ally?
I stand convicted of impiety,
the evidence my pious duty done.
Should the gods think that this is righteousness,
in suffering I'll see my error clear.
But if it is the others who are wrong
I wish them no greater punishment than mine.

Chorus

> The same tempest of mind
> as ever, controls the girl.   930

Creon

> Therefore her guards shall regret
> the slowness with which they move.

Antigone

> That word comes close to death.

Creon

> You are perfectly right in that.

Antigone

> O town of my fathers in Thebe's land,
> O gods of our house.
> I am led away at last.
> Look, leaders of Thebes,   940
> I am last of your royal line.
> Look what I suffer, at whose command,
> because I respected the right.

> *(Antigone is led away. The slow procession should begin during
> the preceding passage.)*

Chorus

> Danaë suffered too.
> She went from the light to the brass-built room,
> chamber and tomb together. Like you, poor child,
> she was of great descent, and more, she held and kept
> the seed of the golden rain which was Zeus.   950
> Fate has terrible power.
> You cannot escape it by wealth or war.
> No fort will keep it out, no ships outrun it.

> Remember the angry king,
> son of Dryas, who raged at the god and paid,
> pent in a rock-walled prison. His bursting wrath
> slowly went down. As the terror of madness went,
> he learned of his frenzied attack on the god.   960
> Fool, he had tried to stop
> the dancing women possessed of god,
> the fire of Dionysus, the songs and flutes.

> Where the dark rocks divide
> sea from sea in Thrace
> is Salmydessus whose savage god   970

beheld the terrible blinding wounds
dealt to Phineus' sons by their father's wife.
Dark the eyes that looked to avenge their mother.
Sharp with her shuttle she struck, and blooded her hands.

Wasting they wept their fate,
settled when they were born   980
to Cleopatra, unhappy queen.
She was a princess too, of an ancient house,
reared in the cave of the wild north wind, her father.
Half a goddess but, child, she suffered like you.

> *(Enter, from the side Teiresias, the blind prophet,*
> *led by a boy attendant.)*

Teiresias

Elders of Thebes, we two have come one road,
two of us looking through one pair of eyes.
This is the way of walking for the blind.   990

Creon

Teiresias, what news has brought you here?

Teiresias

I'll tell you. You in turn must trust the prophet.

Creon

I've always been attentive to your counsel.

Teiresias

And therefore you have steered this city straight.

Creon

So I can say how helpful you have been.

Teiresias

But now you are balanced on a razor's edge.

Creon

What is it? How I shudder at your words!

Teiresias

You'll know, when you hear the signs that I have marked
I sat where every bird of heaven comes   1000

in my old place of augury, and heard
bird-cries I'd never known. They screeched about
goaded by madness, inarticulate.
I marked that they were tearing one another
with claws of murder. I could hear the wing-beats.
I was afraid, so straight away I tried
burnt sacrifice upon the flaming altar.
No fire caught my offerings. Slimy ooze
dripped on the ashes, smoked and sputtered there.
Gall burst its bladder, vanished into vapor;   1010
the fat dripped from the bones and would not burn.
These are the omens of the rites that failed,
as my boy here has told me. He's my guide
as I am guide to others.
Why has this sickness struck against the state?
Through your decision.
All of the altars of the town are choked
with leavings of the dogs and birds; their feast
was on that fated, fallen Polyneices.
So the gods will have no offering from us,
not prayer, nor flame of sacrifice. The birds   1020
will not cry out a sound I can distinguish,
gorged with the greasy blood of that dead man.
Think of these things, my son. All men may err
but error once committed, he's no fool
nor yet unfortunate, who gives up his stiffness
and cures the trouble he has fallen in.
Stubbornness and stupidity are twins.
Yield to the dead. Why goad him where he lies?
What use to kill the dead a second time?   1030
I speak for your own good. And I am right.
Learning from a wise counsellor is not pain
if what he speaks are profitable words.

Creon
Old man, you all, like bowmen at a mark,
have bent your bows at me. I've had my share

of seers. I've been an item in your accounts.
Make profit, trade in Lydian silver-gold,
pure gold of India; that's your chief desire.
But you will never cover up that corpse.
Not if the very eagles tear their food   1040
from him, and leave it at the throne of Zeus.
I wouldn't give him up for burial
in fear of that pollution. For I know
no mortal being can pollute the gods.
O old Teiresias, human beings fall;
the clever ones the furthest, when they plead
a shameful case so well in hope of profit.

Teiresias
Alas!
What man can tell me, has he thought at all . . .

Creon
What hackneyed saw is coming from your lips?

Teiresias
How better than all wealth is sound good counsel.   1050

Creon
And so is folly worse than anything.

Teiresias
And you're infected with that same disease.

Creon
I'm reluctant to be uncivil to a seer . . .

Teiresias
You're that already. You have said I lie.

Creon
Well, the whole crew of seers are money-mad.

Teiresias
And the whole tribe of tyrants grab at gain.

Creon
Do you realize you are talking to a king?

Teiresias

    I know. Who helped you save this town you hold?

Creon

    You're a wise seer, but you love wickedness.

Teiresias

    You'll bring me to speak the unspeakable, very soon.   1060

Creon

    Well, speak it out. But do not speak for profit.

Teiresias

    No, there's no profit in my words for you.

Creon

    You'd better realise that you can't deliver
    my mind, if you should sell it, to the buyer.

Teiresias

    Know well, the sun will not have rolled its course
    many more days, before you come to give
    corpse for these corpses, child of your own loins.
    For you've confused the upper and lower worlds.
    You sent a life to settle in a tomb;
    you keep up here that which belongs below   1070
    the corpse unburied, robbed of its release.
    Not you, nor any god that rules on high
    can claim him now.
    You rob the nether gods of what is theirs.
    So the pursuing horrors lie in wait
    to track you down. The Furies sent by Hades
    and by all gods will even you with your victims.
    Now say that I am bribed! At no far time
    shall men and women wail within your house.
    And all the cities that you fought in war   1080
    whose sons had burial from wild beasts, or dogs,
    or birds that brought the stench of your great wrong
    back to each hearth, they move against you now.
    A bowman, as you said, I send my shafts,

now you have moved me, straight. You'll feel the wound.
Boy, take me home now. Let him spend his rage
on younger men, and learn to calm his tongue,
and keep a better mind than now he does.   1090

(*Exit.*)

Chorus

Lord, he has gone. Terrible prophecies!
And since the time when I first grew grey hair
his sayings to the city have been true.

Creon

I also know this. And my mind is torn.
To yield is dreadful. But to stand against him.
Dreadful to strike my spirit to destruction.

Chorus

Now you must come to counsel, and take advice.

Creon

What must I do? Speak, and I shall obey.

Chorus

Go free the maiden from that rocky house.   1100
Bury the dead who lies in readiness.

Creon

This is your counsel? You would have me yield?

Chorus

Quick as you can. The gods move very fast
when they bring ruin on misguided men.

Creon

How hard, abandonment of my desire.
But I can fight necessity no more.

Chorus

Do it yourself. Leave it to no one else.

Creon

I'll go at once. Come, followers, to your work.
You that are here round up the other fellows.

Take axes with you, hurry to that place
that overlooks us.   1110
Now my decision has been overturned
shall I, who bound her, set her free myself.
I've come to fear it's best to hold the laws
of old tradition to the end of life.

                                          (*Exit.*)

Chorus

God of the many names, Semele's golden child,
child of Olympian thunder, Italy's lord.
Lord of Eleusis, where all men come   1120
to mother Demeter's plain.
Bacchus, who dwell in Thebes,
by Ismenus' running water,
where wild Bacchic women are at home,
on the soil of the dragon seed.

Seen in the glaring flame, high on the double mount,
with the nymphs of Parnassus at play on the hill,
seen by Kastalia's flowing stream.   1130
You come from the ivied heights,
from green Euboea's shore.
In immortal words we cry
your name, lord, who watch the ways,
the many ways of Thebes.

This is your city, honored beyond the rest,
the town of your mother's miracle-death.
Now, as we wrestle our grim disease,   1140
come with healing step from Parnassus' slope
or over the moaning sea.

Leader in dance of the fire-pulsing stars,
overseer of the voices of night,
child of Zeus, be manifest,
with due companionship of Maenad maids   1150
whose cry is but your name.

          (*Enter one of those who left with Creon, as messenger.*)

Messenger

Neighbors of Cadmus, and Amphion's house,
there is no kind of state in human life
which I now dare to envy or to blame.
Luck sets it straight, and luck she overturns
the happy or unhappy day by day.
No prophecy can deal with men's affairs.   1160
Creon was envied once, as I believe,
for having saved this city from its foes
and having got full power in this land.
He steered it well. And he had noble sons.
Now everything is gone.
Yes, when a man has lost all happiness,
he's not alive. Call him a breathing corpse.
Be very rich at home. Live as a king.
But once your joy has gone, though these are left
they are smoke's shadow to lost happiness.   1170

Chorus

What is the grief of princes that you bring?

Messenger

They're dead. The living are responsible.

Chorus

Who died? Who did the murder? Tell us now.

Messenger

Haemon is gone. One of his kin drew blood.

Chorus

But whose arm struck? His father's or his own?

Messenger

He killed himself. His blood is on his father.

Chorus

Seer, all too true the prophecy you told!

Messenger

This is the state of things. Now make your plans.

(*Enter, from the palace, Eurydice.*)

Chorus

    Eurydice is with us now, I see.   1180

    Creon's poor wife. She may have come by chance.

    She may have heard something about her son.

Eurydice

    I heard your talk as I was coming out

    to greet the goddess Pallas with my prayer.

    And as I moved the bolts that held the door

    I heard of my own sorrow.

    I fell back fainting in my women's arms.

    But say again just what the news you bring.   1190

    I, whom you speak to, have known grief before.

Messenger

    Dear lady, I was there, and I shall tell,

    leaving out nothing of the true account.

    Why should I make it soft for you with tales

    to prove myself a liar? Truth is right.

    I followed your husband to the plain's far edge,

    where Polyneices' corpse was lying still

    unpitied. The dogs had torn him all apart.   1200

    We prayed the goddess of all journeyings,

    and Pluto, that they turn their wrath to kindness,

    we gave the final purifying bath,

    then burned the poor remains on new-cut boughs,

    and heaped a high mound of his native earth.

    Then turned we to the maiden's rocky bed,

    death's hollow marriage-chamber.

    But, still far off, one of us heard a voice

    in keen lament by that unblest abode.

    He ran and told the master. As Creon came

    he heard confusion crying. He groaned and spoke: 1210

    "Am I a prophet now, and do I tread

    the saddest of all roads I ever trod?

    My son's voice crying! Servants, run up close,

stand by the tomb and look, push through the crevice
where we built the pile of rock, right to the entry.
Find out if that is Haemon's voice I hear
or if the gods are tricking me indeed."
We obeyed the order of our mournful master.
In the far corner of the tomb we saw   1220
her, hanging by the neck, caught in a noose
of her own linen veiling.
Haemon embraced her as she hung, and mourned
his bride's destruction, dead and gone below,
his father's actions, the unfated marriage.
When Creon saw him, he groaned terribly,
and went toward him, and called him with lament:
"What have you done, what plan have you caught up,
what sort of suffering is killing you?
Come out, my child, I do beseech you, come!"   1230
The boy looked at him with his angry eyes,
spat in his face and spoke no further word.
He drew his sword, but as his father ran,
he missed his aim. Then the unhappy boy,
in anger at himself, leant on the blade.
It entered, half its length, into his side.
While he was conscious he embraced the maiden,
holding her gently. Last, he gasped out blood,
red blood on her white cheek.
Corpse on a corpse he lies. He found his marriage.   1240
Its celebration in the halls of Hades.
So he has made it very clear to men
that to reject good counsel is a crime.

(Eurydice returns to the house.)

Chorus

What do you make of this? The queen has gone
in silence. We know nothing of her mind.

Messenger

I wonder at her, too. But we can hope
that she has gone to mourn her son within

with her own women, not before the town.
She knows discretion. She will do no wrong.   1250

Chorus

I am not sure. This muteness may portend
as great disaster as a loud lament.

Messenger

I will go in and see if some deep plan
hides in her heart's wild pain. You may be right.
There can be heavy danger in mute grief.

> (*The messenger goes into the house. Creon enters with his
> followers. They are carrying Haemon's body on a bier.*)

Chorus

But look, the king draws near.
His own hand brings
the witness of his crime,
the doom he brought on himself.   1260

Creon

O crimes of my wicked heart,
harshness bringing death.
You see the killer, you see the kin he killed.
My planning was all unblest.
Son, you have died too soon.
Oh, you have gone away
through my fault, not your own.

Chorus

You have learned justice, though it comes too late.   1270

Creon

Yes, I have learned in sorrow. It was a god who struck,
who has weighted my head with disaster; he drove me to wild
    strange ways,
his heavy heel on my joy.
Oh sorrows, sorrows of men.

> (*Re-enter the messenger, from a side door of the palace.*)

Messenger

    Master, you hold one sorrow in your hands
    but you have more, stored up inside the house.   1280

Creon

    What further suffering can come on me?

Messenger

    Your wife has died. The dead man's mother in deed,
    poor soul, her wounds are fresh.

Creon

    Hades, harbor of all,
    you have destroyed me now.
    Terrible news to hear, horror the tale you tell.   1290
    I was dead, and you kill me again.
    Boy, did I hear you right?
    Did you say the queen was dead,
    slaughter on slaughter heaped?

                    (The central doors of the palace begin to open.)

Chorus

    Now you can see. Concealment is all over.

           (The doors are open, and the corpse of Eurydice is revealed.)

Creon

    My second sorrow is here. Surely no fate remains
    which can strike me again. Just now, I held my son in my arms.
    And now I see her dead.
    Woe for the mother and son.   1300

Messenger

    There, by the altar, dying on the sword,
    her eyes fell shut. She wept her older son
    who died before, and this one. Last of all
    she cursed you as the killer of her children.

Creon

    I am mad with fear. Will no one strike
    and kill me with cutting sword?
    Sorrowful, soaked in sorrow to the bone!   1310

Messenger

    Yes, for she held you guilty in the death
    of him before you, and the elder dead.

Creon

    How did she die?

Messenger

               Struck home at her own heart
    when she had heard of Haemon's suffering.

Creon

    This is my guilt, all mine. I killed you, I say it clear.
    Servants, take me away, out of the sight of men.   1320
    I who am nothing more than nothing now.

Chorus

    Your plan is good—if any good is left.
    Best to cut short our sorrow.

Creon

    Let me go, let me go. May death come quick,
    bringing my final day.   1330
    O let me never see tomorrow's dawn.

Chorus

    That is the future's. We must look to now.
    What will be is in other hands than ours.

Creon

    All my desire was in that prayer of mine.

Chorus

    Pray not again. No mortal can escape
    the doom prepared for him.

Creon

    Take me away at once, the frantic man who killed   1340
    my son, against my meaning. I cannot rest.
    My life is warped past cure. My fate has struck me down.

            (Creon and his attendants enter the house.)

Chorus

> Our happiness depends
> on wisdom all the way.
> The gods must have their due.
> Great words by men of pride
> bring greater blows upon them.
> So wisdom comes to the old.

1350

A NOTE ON THE TEXT

THE foregoing is a translation of the text of Jebb's third edition (Cambridge, 1900). In the dialogue, I have tried to bring into English almost all that I thought I saw in the Greek, even though this was to run the risk of a clumsy literalism. In the choruses, I have taken more freedom.

The following are the places where my rendering is of another text than Jebb's.

486 ὁμαιμονεστέρας A, other MSS, and the scholiast in L. ὁμαιμονεστέρα L, as corrected from -αις, Jebb.

The extravagance of imagining the impossible possibility of closer blood kin than a sister seems to me in character for Creon at this point. (For a similar use of language, cf. Aeschylus *Septem* 197.)

519 τούτους MSS and Jebb. ἴσους is recorded by L's scholiast and read by Pearson. Line 520 seems even more pointed if Creon is picking up Antigone's own term to throw at her.

572. This line is Ismene's in all the manuscripts. The only traditional evidence for giving it to Antigone is that the Aldine edition (1502) and Turnebus (1553) gave it to her. These editors may have had manuscript evidence lost to us. But they may also, like most modern editors, including Jebb, have been exercising their own sense of fitness. It is touching to have an Antigone stung from her silence to defend her lover. Further, if the line is not hers, we are faced with an Antigone who never mentions him; and much has been built on this.

The best argument for giving her the line is Creon's reply to it (573). If Ismene has 572 "your marriage" must mean "the marriage you talk of," or words to that effect. This is possible, but the phrase would certainly come out more naturally to Antigone.

Confusions of speakers in stichomythia are many, and I see no possibility of certainty here. It is our misfortune that the line in question is an important one. I have stayed with the manuscripts, which seems to me all one can do.

574. This is Ismene's line in all MSS. Boeckh, followed by Jebb, gave it to the chorus. I have followed my own precedent in 572, and stayed with the MSS. The question might come, as Jebb argues, more reasonably from the chorus than from Ismene, who has had her answer already. But she is not too logical to ask the same appalling question twice.

600 κόνις MSS, Jebb. κοπίς Reiske and others, Jebb in earlier editions, Pearson. See Jebb's note and appendix. He was of two minds here. My own final feeling is that for dust to be doing the reaping is too much, even for a tragic chorus.

609 παντογήρως L, the MSS generally, L's scholiast. παντ᾽ ἀγρεύων, Jebb. This image was too strained for Jebb (and many others), as the dust in 600 was for me. De gustibus. . . .

904–20. Jebb (following and followed by many) brackets these lines, which are in all the MSS, and were known to Aristotle as Antigone's. I think he is wrong, but he should not be pilloried as a prudish Victorian for this. The positions of his note and appendix are well taken and held. Some sensible contemporaries (e.g., Fitts and Fitzgerald) are with him still. For those, like myself, who are sure the lines are Antigone's, there is drama in her abandoning her moralities and clinging to her irrational profundity of feeling for her lost and irreplaceable brother, devising legalistic arguments for her intellectual justification. Jebb finds the syntax of 909–12 strained past all bearing, but I believe Antigone's obscurity here a touch of realism parallel to the confused and contradictory negatives of her opening lines, which Jebb allows her.